TranscenDANCE—Lessons from Living, Loving, and Dancing

By

Melissa Drake

To license this content or purchase in bulk, please email Melissa Drake at melissa@uncorpedinfluence.com or visit uncorpedinfluence.com.

Thank you for purchasing TranscenDANCE. Download a free frameable summary of TranscenDANCE concepts here: bit.ly/FreeTranscenDANCEPrint

ISBN 978-1-7346543-0-1 E-Book (Mobi)
ISBN 978-1-7346543-1-8 Paperback (P.O.D.)
ISBN 978-1-7346543-2-5 Paperback (offset)
ISBN 978-1-7346543-3-2 E-Book (ePub)

Praise for *TranscenDANCE*

We need this book. I need this book. It's an excellent story full of hope and overcoming hardships that inspires you to look both out to the Universe and within, that also makes you want to get up and move through life and across the dance floor!

TranscenDANCE makes the idea of therapy so real, actionable, and tangible. It's proof we can do the work through different avenues. It's a call to connect with ourselves and the outer world through dance. It's a reminder that the Universe has our back and we have the tools and abilities to get up and live a beautiful life.

We need to keep opening up the world of self-care, mental health and dealing with life. This thought—the movement of TranscenDANCE—inspires that. This book provokes us to transcend above the belief that psychology, mental health, and therapy are about someone telling us how to live our lives and putting us in a box so we're all the same kind of "normal."

This theory, coupled with Melissa's story, adds color to our beautiful minds and to the way we choose to move through life. It gives even more power to the connection people feel with music and dance, and how they make us feel alive.

—Linda Gordon

I absolutely love, love, love this book!! There is so much in it that I want to share with my family and friends! It's so relatable, honest, and fun. Truly a fantastic story of how to rise above your own bullshit and become who you were born to be! All while dancing the night away!

—Sue Thompson

I think TranscenDANCE speaks to spiritual strength and emotional perseverance. I think it also speaks to vulnerability and the willingness to live one's best life, no matter what. Melissa writes over and over about hitting barriers, bearing judgments, and becoming weary under the various pressures of her life. Some of her experiences would've felled less spiritually-minded folk. But not her, because she also writes about overcoming obstacles, unshackling herself from judgment (from within and without), and rallying to stay steady in her cause to uplift others by collaborating with them and by sharing her deeply personal story. Melissa's readiness to try new things and to find joy, despite the pain, is truly inspirational. Her fortitude is a profound reminder that no matter what we do, if we can simply trust in the Universe and the Dance it lays before us, we can accomplish our wildest dreams.

– Sean Cardinalli

This is a very unique book because it uses the language of dance to connect the dots to personal growth. The experiences shared are honest and, much like dancing, create an atmosphere of inclusion. When reading this book, I could often see the parallels to my own experiences and found new meaning and understanding of my past to better prepare for my future. Now, I see the connection between dancing, martial arts and surfing.

One of the best ways to learn is from someone who speaks to you in terms that you can understand and relate to, and everyone can relate to some form of dancing. Dancing has been an integrated part of the human experience, arguably since the very beginning. There are some people who communicate better thru dancing than with spoken words.

No matter what your preferred style of dancing, it can create joy, reunite you with a feeling of value, and increase your self-esteem. Sometimes that first half-step is the hardest; give this book chance to dance its way into your library.

—Eric Cedeno

Acknowledgements

I'm grateful for the safe haven of teen dance clubs that introduced me to dance at the age of 14. Huge thanks to my friends Valerie and Stephanie, and my cousin David for frequenting them with me. Big shout out to Valerie for the hair flips and introducing me to the best women's restroom in San Diego's Gaslamp District at Parq—it has a **bar** in the women's restroom.

I'll forever be grateful to Nicole for my first stint with dancing "back in the day" **and** my recovery dancing in the later years. The immense number of inside jokes we share about those times, and the stories about going back and forth and back and forth from club to club to club on Court Avenue are tucked safely in my heart. I'll never forget the forever full moon and the second weekend of the month. Love you, man!

Huge thanks to Beverly for getting me out of the house after my crippling depression came on and for taking me on my first dance outing after I lost my parents. You helped me find my wings and I'm forever grateful.

Laurie—I can't thank you enough for reaching out to me via Facebook messenger and beginning what was to become a beautiful relationship and dance journey for us. Silver Becky—you have the biggest heart. Thank you for sharing it with me and all the other Smart Wild Kinky Mamas.

Everyone needs a friend like Eric Cedeno. You'll understand why when you read the book. I'm so grateful our paths crossed at Camp Xanadu in the fall of 2019. I value your feedback and treasure the way you encouraged and cheered me on.

Sean Kubota, thank you for showing me what passion in action is and what pushing the limits of desire looks like. Thank you for demonstrating a kick-ass way to launch your book, *Victim to Hero*, and all the goodness of your Give Thanks event. Thanks to you, I'm claiming my epic!

Knowing my story through Facebook, and being acquainted with our coaching and editing process, my talented friend Marcos Cervantes III suggested *TranscenDANCE* as the title for the book. Words are incredibly important to me and I love the way *TranscenDANCE* reflects a healing journey through dance. Thank you, Marcos from the bottom of my heart.

Thank you to Denny Arthur for providing a safe place for adults over 30 to connect and get down.

I so appreciate the plethora of events in California that offer dance venues and perspectives I've never seen before.

I appreciate my California friends Aileen, Cathy, Janae, Jodi, Lillian, Mark, Tina, and Sean for being in-person supports, helping me find new places to dance, and joining me under the disco ball.

Stephen Thomas, you are a fun and energetic dance instructor and performer. Private lessons with you have helped me understand and transcend ineffective patterns through dance. Your patience, expertise, and abundant humor is appreciated.

Thank you to my online and long-distance friends for supporting my journey and holding my hand through my trials and tribulations as I struggled to find my voice and put my work out there. Beth and Vanessa, you have my heart.

Sean Cardinalli, my friend and my editor. I'm so glad Facebook and personal travels brought us together. Thank you for holding me and this book to the highest literary and storytelling standards. Your expertise with screenwriting, dance, and recovery programs were the perfect combination to really take this book to the next level.

Thank you to Sue Thompson for being the friend and chosen family who supported me through all stages of my TranscenDANCE. I appreciate the safe communication we share and your demonstration of effective boundaries and of living life "in the gray" for greater satisfaction.

To my son, Johnathan—thank you for supporting my journey, following my imperfect lead all the way to California, and learning new dances with me. I appreciate the way you always give your best on the dance floor and in our relationship. I love you with all my heart and appreciate you more than you know.

To my future love—there's so much love here. I'm preparing to follow your lead. I promise to mirror your movement and reflect your light while shining as brightly as I can. Our thriving connection will provide mutual support as we individually flourish and our radiated love provides collective benefit. I can't wait to share space with you, exchange sacred energy, and enjoy the dance of our lives.

Foreword

I am most honored to write this foreword for *TranscenDANCE* by Melissa Drake. From the moment I met Melissa, as a guest at one of my social dances, I knew there was something extraordinary and special about her. At the time, I had no idea of the specifics or magnitude of her attributes, and what was going to come of our interaction in the very near future. I didn't imagine that a year later she would commence private dancing lessons with me, and that our personalities would click in that first dance lesson.

From that very first meeting, and the first dance lesson a year later, it was apparent that Melissa was unlike any student I taught before. She understood and related to my approach and philosophies to dancing, which are based on principles of connection, movement, energy, dynamics, and human interaction.

From the very beginning of her training in dance, I explained my thoughts that partner dancing is a form of communication between two people, which has the potential to connect mind, body, and soul, while reacting to each other's energy, gestures, feelings and intentions. Of course, I have explained this to many students before, but it is extremely rare that a student embraces it 100 percent from the very first lesson.

Unbeknownst to me at that time, "therapy" through partner dance was exactly what Melissa was seeking in her journey in life. It seems the Universe brought us both together to achieve this focus. Melissa, apparently, was already allowing the Universe to lead!

I was so impressed that following our first dance lessons, she would go home, analyze the content of the lessons, and write to me summarizing all the points—doing so better than I could myself. It was immediately apparent that Melissa possesses the rare qualities and skills of being able to make connections, connect the dots, and relate principles which are obviously related, but which to other people may seem unrelatable. I had no idea Melissa's initial notes were the start of her writing this extraordinary book.

Melissa absolutely nails the dance concepts in *TranscenDANCE*. She brings together all the benefits of dance and all the principles of connection, lead-and-follow, teamwork, and interaction between people; all the necessary components needed to reach full potential in relating, connecting, and working together. Her stories, experiences, observations, and feelings are highly relatable. While reading this book, I kept telling myself, "That's happened to me," and "That's how I feel." Through her stories and explanation, Melissa teaches readers how they can deal with the myriad situations we all experience in life.

Most importantly, in *TranscenDANCE*, Melissa demonstrates the power of dance and the application of the dynamics that make dancing the ultimate interpersonal experience. This book is a demonstration of what she and I believe to be the best form of therapy in overcoming all sorts of predicaments and ailments, including depression. Ultimately, Melissa presents us with all the principles and insights to allow the Universe to lead!

—Stephen Thomas, Fellow of The Associated Board of Dance (ABD), professional dancer and owner of Stephen Thomas Dance

Table of Contents

When you dance,
you can enjoy
the luxury of being you.
— Paulo Coelho
TranscenDANCE

Introduction

Have you experienced "the luxury of being you?" I was 43-years-old before I even considered being myself; let alone fully owning who I am. It seems that years of conditioning, people-pleasing, and suppressing my true desires at my own expense left me in a place of playing many roles, none of which were me. Worse, the continual suppression and repression of my **self** resulted in severe depression that plagued me throughout most of my life. To be honest, I'm not sure the real me has fully emerged, but she's certainly evolving and I'm so grateful.

It takes courage to consistently show up as just me and I can't say I have my place in the world completely figured out. The more I learn, the more I understand that my attempts to crack life's code and control everything are the very things that keep me from emerging in all my glory. The more I wield control, the less I experience it, and the farther away I get from the luxury of being me.

Here's part of the luxury of being me: I can drop all pretenses. I don't have to cover up my flaws, wear a mask, or pretend to be something I'm not. At the same time, being me frees me from the need to apologize for who I am and who I am not. As me, there's nothing to prove, nothing to earn, and nothing to compensate for. Being me is as easy—and challenging—as breathing.

From the moment we're born, we breathe without a thought and are sustained. It's easy and effortless. Yet, oftentimes, our breath becomes shallow and unregulated due to anxiety, anger, shock, or fright. In those scenarios, we don't experience the true benefits of each breath. It's like we forget to just breathe and be who we are. Being yourself is the same way. Sometimes, in certain situations, we don't show up as ourselves; we're wearing a disguise born of insecurity, fear, trauma, or distrust, and we forget to just be—that is, to just breathe and let our guard down. When that happens, we neglect to appreciate the benefits of the Universal forces that sustain us and make us, us. Instead, life becomes a cursory experiment that keeps us guessing, searching, and self-loathing, rather than one that drives, enlivens, and elevates us.

Showing up on purpose, for a purpose, engages the support of the Universe. However, most people live from a place of scarcity, where they hide their talents in favor of the "comforts" of a steady routine, paycheck, and relations. I'm guilty of this, too! I think this happens because sometimes it's hard to fathom the abundance of the Universe we live in. Conditioning suppresses a sense of wonder. It's so easy to get caught up in day-to-day life and in making a living, and to fail to remember what it's like to experience joy. Worse, there's no time set aside to dance. I absolutely love this quote from Gabrielle Roth about the connection between mental health and dancing:

> In many shamanic societies, if you came to a medicine person complaining of being disheartened, dispirited, or depressed, they would ask one of four questions: "When did you stop dancing? When did you stop singing? When did you stop being enchanted by stories? When did you stop being comforted by the sweet territory of silence?"

No doubt, the shamans are onto something. When we acknowledge the forces of life's dance and work with them, in-time, in rhythm; when we show up as ourselves and enjoy the Universe's choreography, magic unfolds. We are no longer going against the rhythm and we aren't alone, dancing with ourselves like Billy Idol, but instead enlivened and present.

Tapping into a life that sustains us requires trust and belief in something greater than us. Call it God, call it Spirit, call it the Universe, or Higher Power, but know this: **we are led by it**. Better said, the Universe **wants** to lead us, with love and compassion, through the dance, to help us manifest our truest and most honest desires. Often, however, we're so busy in our heads, out of the present moment, and into our ego controlling things, we miss the subtle lead, we stumble over our steps; we try to lead instead of being led, and we ignore the invitation to enjoy the dance of our lives.

Eckhart Tolle's famous quote, "Life is the dancer and you are the dance" sums up TranscenDANCE perfectly. When we trust our intuition and follow the lead the Universe offers as we live our lives, the resulting dance is our unique expression and offering to the world. Life offers a lead. Those with the openness, courage, stamina, and resilience to follow the lead are rewarded with the luxury of being themselves.

In my attempt to allow myself to be led by the Universe as the most powerful and graceful dance partner—to stop bouncing around aimlessly, stepping on toes—I enrolled in private dance lessons. I met Stephen Thomas a year or more before at a dance event I found on Facebook. He's a pro dancer from Australia with 30 years' experience as a competitor and performer. I knew from the first time I met him at a group lesson, I'd work with him again. He's not only incredibly knowledgeable and knows dance inside and out, he's got amazing moves, a sense of humor, and a heart that shines. We followed each other on social media after our first meeting and stayed in touch.

I reached out for private lessons after moving into my own California apartment in the summer of 2019. After I trekked cross-country from Des Moines, Iowa in 2017, I was very happy and proud to finally have a place of my own. (My first two years in California, I lived in a house with three adult roommates.) As grateful as I was to have my own luxury apartment for the first time in California, I was also incredibly lonely and disheartened. I didn't know a soul in my new town of Fullerton. Living alone and working from home took a toll on me. I was ready to connect with others and commit to living out my purpose with the lead of the Universe rather than controlling, resisting, and denying it.

The dance lessons proved to be the greatest therapy I've ever experienced. In fact, I made a purposeful choice to pursue dance lessons over more traditional therapy. There's something about body movement, music, and rhythm, that helps me think in new ways. I have an uncanny ability to relate seemingly unrelated things, and dancing certainly helps with this flow. For some, this "clearing out the ego" process happens in the shower, or while driving, or during meditation, or right at the cusp of sleep at night. But for me, the Universe's possibilities—in me—were discovered via dance. In the chapters of this book, I'll walk you through my dance journey, share what I learned from dance, and explain the conclusions that help me enjoy the luxury of being me.

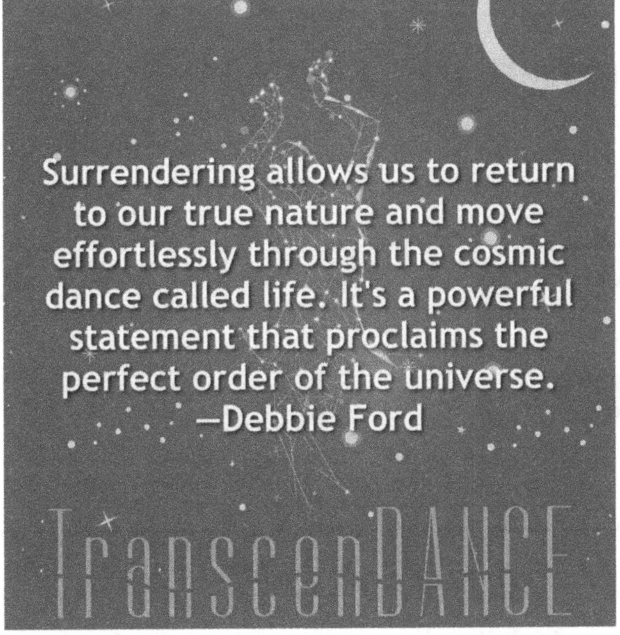
Surrendering allows us to return
to our true nature and move
effortlessly through the cosmic
dance called life. It's a powerful
statement that proclaims the
perfect order of the universe.
—Debbie Ford
TranscenDANCE

Chapter 1

Letting the Universe Lead

TranscenDANCE is the process of surrendering to the lead of the Universe. It's a deep knowing, a resonance of unwavering faith, and a compelling pull forward to your highest calling. It's being poised to dance with life as it comes. It's remaining present, staying in the moment, and navigating life one step at a time. It's knowing each move and opening is created for the highest good of all parties. It's allowing the Universe to move through you and expressing your true self.

TranscenDANCE requires trust and faith beyond any you've ever experienced. It's a slow, deep unravelling of everything you've known to reveal the greatest inner brilliance you can imagine. This light is your soul within, once dimmed by expectations, conditioning, contrasting situations, limiting beliefs, bullshit rules, and incessant fears. The more you surrender to the unknown while maintaining your soul's center, moving with grace, and staying in joy, the easier it is to accept and follow the lead of the Universe.

TranscenDANCE requires periods of movement and rest to shed layer upon layer of indoctrination, self-sabotage, and patterns that do not serve your development. This healing will challenge and test you to make sure you're resilient and able to sustain your life's huge calling. At the point you think you'll break down, you'll surrender more, and you'll break *through*.

TranscenDANCE is a process of honoring the dark, embracing your shadow, and accepting your imperfections in order to shine more brightly. For a long time, I chose not to acknowledge my darkness and imperfections—not realizing they were completely visible to everyone but me. This led to a very disjointed life and a failure to accept myself, my past, and my purpose. I learned that it's not possible to remain healthy while denying myself. Failing to care for myself while ignoring my passion kept me in an endless cycle of dis-ease. In order to fly, I had to surrender to the process. Essentially, TransenDANCE is metamorphosis akin to a caterpillar becoming a butterfly.

> Butterflies, bees
> our wingèd, happy friends
> Oh, to dance in the air
> and float on the breeze...
> —Terri Guillemets

Transcend [tran-send] (from dictonary.com)
verb

1. to rise above or go beyond; overpass; exceed: to transcend the limits of thought; kindness transcends courtesy.
2. to outdo or exceed in excellence, elevation, extent, degree, etc.; surpass; excel.
3. to be above and independent of (the universe, time, etc.).

TranscenDANCE
noun

1. to rise above and go beyond personal expectations, limiting beliefs, and disparaging patterns through dance.
2. to transmute trauma through body movement.
3. to leverage dance themes in order to connect with, rely on, and trust in the ever-present Universal supports.

People who've completed TranscenDANCE are open to receive, allowing the gifts of life's flow, appreciating every offering, and then asking for more. They know with certainty they're worthy of receiving everything they desire and more. They move with freedom and fluidity surrendering to and relying on the lead of the Universe.

Just like fun dance parties infused with great music, amazing friends, and snacks galore, this book is supported by proven methods to support your personal TransenDANCE. At the end of each chapter, you'll find prompts and related playlists to help you dance through and integrate what you've learned. Special thanks to Vanessa Sandberg for leading the chapter prompts.

Speaking of dancing through this book, there will be places throughout where I have "squirrel moments" and share an anecdote that may seem unrelated or off track. These fun facts are indicated as a "Free Spin." When paired with the Universe and other dance partners, it's okay to be unconventional and do our own thing. In dance, a free spin is one that's done without partner contact. They're generally brief expressions before returning to partner dance. In this book, Free Spins will be short tangents that are slightly off track, but relevant to the discussion.

Keep in mind, TranscenDANCE is a process and I've not "arrived." One of my favorite quotes from Abraham Hicks is, "You can't get it wrong and you never get it done." As much as I want to get "there," I appreciate knowing life is an endless dance with more steps, turns, and routines to enjoy throughout the experience. I've learned many lessons through dance. I appreciate the way dance enriches my life. I'm most excited to realize my future desired life and dance where I'm led, supported, and thriving.

Let's dance!!

TranscenDANCE

Be present and available for the inevitable lead of the Universe.

TranscenDANCE statement:	Transcending current limiting beliefs requires grounding and an ability to trust in the unknown. To release our thoughts and be present in the moment, grounding through meditation is a way to build a foundation where the mind and body connect to Universal support and guidance.
TranscenDANCE prompt:	Meditate using this nature meditation for relaxation by Body & Brain Meditation to ground yourself and prepare for TranscenDANCE. bit.ly/BBNatureMeditation
TranscenDANCE Spotify playlist:	**The Universe Leads** bit.ly/TheUniverseLeadsPlaylist Whenever you're feeling doubt and need a reminder that the Universe is on your side and ready to lead your dance with life, give this playlist a listen.

Dance first. Think later.
It's the natural order.
—Samuel Beckett
TranscenDANCE

Chapter 2

Dance Levels, Locations, and Times

I talked with someone recently who exclaimed, “So you’re a dancer!” I instinctively replied, “I’m not a dancer.” This person cajoled me saying, “How can you say you’re not a dancer when you’ve written a book about dancing?”

Here’s the thing: I’ve accepted this notion that dancers are people who fit a certain mold. The shape of a dancer looks much different than the way I look. I think of dancers as people who dedicated their whole lives to dancing. Dancers know dance intimately, and the dance community knows them. None of those things applies to me. Yet, as the person asserted, I am undeniably a dancer. I’m also one who loves to challenge the status quo and hates being put in a box. I appreciate the dichotomy of duality so much.

Like most things in my life, my experience dancing with life isn't linear. I have progressed and evolved over time. However, I've found that big leaps and advances are generally accompanied by a preceding series of experiences coming to an end. Sometimes those events are positive. Many times, they are negative and even traumatic. That's part of the process. As traumatic as some of the events in my dance and life journey have been, I'm truly grateful for **every** experience. I've come to learn that the trick in appreciating and realizing our personal development is in not assigning judgments to events as positive or negative, but instead by being open to the possibility of something new showing up. One of my favorite mantras is "Everything is happening perfectly." Acceptance of that fact has gotten me through some seriously dark times, while giving me hope for the future at the same time.

This book follows my journey to personal wholeness and fulfilment. I'll be the first to tell you, I've not "arrived." And, healing is a lifelong process that requires shedding layer upon layer to unearth a deeper understanding. Unfortunately, healing is not a light switch that's switched on and stays on forever. When I first woke to my healing, I was sure I'd never let my light be dimmed again. However, I was completely unaware of the multitude of layers upon layers I would still have to navigate—and that included repeat visits to darkness as well as light.

Truth be told, a decade ago, I was drowning in my own bullshit, most of which I didn't even know was my issue, let alone my responsibility. The most pivotal turning point for me was working with a new therapist, one I trusted to tell me the truth—especially when I didn't want to hear it. My first session with that therapist was over six years ago. A few years into my recovery and support to become med-free, I claimed a Brilliant Transformation and went about my "recovered" life.

But here's the thing about recovery, awakening, and enlightenment—the process doesn't end. While we may think we've "mastered" a lesson, chances are we will encounter opportunities to level-up that mastery and learn the lesson on a deeper level (time and time again).

In the last year, my personal bullshit became "next level." Next Level Bullshit is often recycled bullshit that comes to light when you're on a healing journey. It's the stuff you thought you were beyond, only it resurfaces, still unprocessed like the corn in the toilet. It's the truth staring you in the face reminding you that no matter how much you've evolved, there will always be work to do and lessons to learn. Apparently, these lessons need to be pulverized before they are released for good. Only, the learning and processing takes place in layers, over decades—and even lifetimes. You'll see evidence of this in my journey to wholeness. As my editor noted, "I was enjoying the highs of these shares and appreciate the lows but the lows are, like, super horror movie-graphic. It's jarring..." Tell me about it!!

Like life and dance, this book isn't exactly linear either. It's a collection of stories related to TranscenDANCE. For clarity, and to help you navigate the journey, I'm providing a general timeline of my progression as a dancer. As someone with ADHD tendencies, I understand how challenging it can be to stay on track—especially with a story that has many twists, turns, and a few shocking admissions. In the chapters that follow, I'll go into detail on my life's events, their implications, and the way they are facilitating my continued TranscenDANCE process. For now, consider the following as an overview of the stages of this progression, not the actual stories of TransenDANCE.

If you're feeling side-tracked, I'm inviting you to stay with me because this is a very interesting and rewarding dance.

Beginning Dance	
Time:	Late 80's to early 90's
Location:	Bars in Des Moines and Marshalltown, Iowa. Most notable clubs: Lucky Lady, Beat Club, Jukebox, and Mike T's.
Atmosphere:	Clubs that opened their doors on Sunday nights to allow underage patrons to have a club experience sans alcohol.
Life Stage:	High Schooler attempting to fit in somewhere.
Appearance:	Thin and beautiful (believing I was fat), totally insecure, and bombarded with messages of not being thin or pretty enough.
Conduct:	Good, clean fun with bits of indecency thrown in for good measure.
Personal Disposition:	Not a care in the world.

I always had a great time dancing. Thankfully, there were a number of clubs in Iowa that opened on Sunday nights to give teenagers a safe place to express themselves. During these teen hours, no alcohol was served and no creepy older folks were allowed in the club. That's not to say we didn't drink before we arrived or hang out with the older crowd after, but in general, we were there to dance. During a senior trip to Dallas, Texas, I secured a fake ID at a flea market and immediately started visiting clubs during regular hours.

After losing my flea market fake, a coworker offered me her birth certificate so I could secure the most legit fake ID possible, (one that included my photo and her information). The only problem? I needed someone to vouch for me. Guess who I brought? My mom. Yes, my mom helped me get a fake ID so I could dance. She later told me she did it because she trusted me and knew I'd be responsible with it. And, for the most part, I *was* responsible. Free Spin: Before all the extreme security and technology at today's DMV, you used to be able to have another person sign for your identity when getting a replacement ID. Shocking, I know!

Using my ID to get into an Urbandale bar called Sneakers, on their all-you-can-drink Wednesday night in June of 1991, I met the man who would later become my husband (after we both had more than we could drink). While we both enjoyed dancing, marriage curbed dancing and many other activities. We separated in November of 1997 and divorced on Christmas Eve, 1998.

A year later, a mutual friend reintroduced me to a high school classmate thinking I could be a supportive mentor for her as she contemplated divorce. Thanks to the introduction, she and I became great friends who danced every other weekend while our kids were at their dad's house. We danced and traveled together with our kids for years. There's something really powerful about single moms connecting. My connection with this person was the first of many single mom dance connections that led me forward.

"Back in the Day" Dancing	
Time:	Late 1990s through 2009
Location:	Bars in Des Moines, Iowa; mostly the Court Avenue bars: Generations, Papa's Planet, The Buzz, Big Kahunas, and Club AM; Coconut Joe's on Wednesday nights, and occasionally Denny Arthur's.
Atmosphere:	A string of downtown clubs where one admittance fee covered all bars. As a VIP, I never waited in line, never paid cover, and the bartender had my drink ready before I danced my way to the bar. An after-hours club was open for dancing until 5 am and we frequently closed it down.
Life Stage:	Single and ready to mingle.
Appearance:	Morbidly obese, heavily made-up, excessively tanned, and owning it.

Conduct:	Unlimited laughs, lots of drinking, and perpetual questionable choices.
Personal Disposition:	Emotionally and physically unconscious.

It wasn't until after my divorce in 1998 that I started dancing again. This multiple-year period began what I called "back in the day" dancing. This dancing was incredibly fun and memorable, but it wasn't transformative in a positive way. Instead, it was an every-other-weekend escape, when my son was at his dad's house. In general, this period of dancing for me centered around binge-drinking and questionable activities. (Except drunk driving, which I've always been adamantly against.) During this time, I was liquored up; dancing was haphazard and often a prelude to casual sex. The casual sexcapades ended when a stranger I brought home killed the mood by threatening to strangle me and leave me for dead. Submitting to him likely saved my life—and ended my desire for casual hook ups.

I vehemently believe women should never be shamed for sexual assault. At the same time, I believe wholeheartedly in the Law of Attraction. Time and distance have shown me the way I attracted this situation through my pursuit of instant gratification and constant numbing, over the pursuit of healing to raise my level of personal consciousness. Because I was emotionally and physically unconscious during this time, there were no personal standards to uphold. And boundaries? I had no concept of them. As a conscious person with boundaries intact, I'm certain I would not have invited that man to my home and the circumstance would not have occurred. Sadly, that incident wasn't enough to wake me up and commit to personal healing yet.

Shortly after the stranger-danger incident, binge-drinking—and consequently dancing—during this period abruptly ended after an alcohol-related injury in 2005. On St. Patrick's Day, I broke my wrist while incredibly drunk. At the time, I had a twice-monthly binge habit. My fall required two surgeries, a permanent screw in my wrist, and a few months in a cast. It also inspired me to slow my drinking. For nearly 10 years, I had the occasional cocktail but never got drunk.

Shortly after I broke my wrist, I slid into a depression which took such a hold that I spent seven years in bed. I literally went to work, did a great job while there, and then came home and got in bed. I was also the poster child for the "sandwich generation" at the time, being a single parent caring for my son, and the primary caregiver for my ailing parents. Dancing happened on occasion, but it was neither a priority nor a desire.

When I lost my mom in August of 2010 and my dad less than a year later, my depression compounded while I sunk deeper into hibernation while becoming less emotionally available as a parent.

A chance meeting with Beverly, the mom of a cheerleader from my son's school, was the first thing that got me out of bed. We were both single moms—she was widowed—and our kids were friends and involved in wresting and football. She invited me out after a Friday night football game. I accepted without a thought and we closed the restaurant down while sharing great conversation and plenty of laughter. From that day forward, she became part of my village and helped me get my footing after my parents' deaths. I later learned that my son was so worried about me and wanted me to get out of the house so badly, that he offered to pay Beverly's gas expenses to pick me up and take me out.

Recovery Dancing	
Time:	Late 2014 through mid-2017
Location:	Bars in Des Moines, Iowa—mostly Denny Arthur's on the weekends and Mickey's on Wednesdays.
Atmosphere:	Dancing among a community of women who supported one another on and off the dance floor.
Life Stage:	New empty nester, recovering from severe depression while managing two chronic illnesses, and adjusting to being recently dismissed from my 25-year career in the insurance industry.
Appearance:	Enjoying a more "palatable" body having lost 110 pounds through chronic illness, ditched the make-up in favor of smiles.
Conduct:	Primary focus on dancing instead of the ancillary shenanigans sometimes associated with dancing in bars.

Personal Disposition:	Starting to find myself and excited about life for the first time in a long time.

When my son left to attend trade school and I became an empty nester, I connected with a group of other empty nesters and single moms through Facebook. We formed a group called Smart Wild Kinky Mamas. This tribe of women supported me through chronic illness, depression recovery, and the loss of my corporate job. Our group of very connected moms talked daily, laughed constantly, danced weekly, and supported one another. We overcame depression, managed divorces and single parenthood, navigated relationships, faced down addictions, and simply became stronger and more beautiful every day.

While this group evolved and dissolved over time, the women I connected with and the lessons I learned from our time together will always hold a special place in my heart.

Conscious and Partner Dancing	
Time:	Late 2017 to present
Location:	Bars and events in the Los Angeles area. Notable clubs include Misty's Lounge, Hamburger Mary's, The Abbey, and The Starting Gate. Event settings included an ocean pier, the beach, a cruise ship, yoga studios, and corporate offices.
Atmosphere:	Truly LA style, which is sometimes weird, often includes live music, crystals, and interesting sights (like half-naked acrobatic women swinging from the ceilings).
Life Stage:	Entrepreneur living and working on my own terms.
Appearance:	Carrying much of the weight I previously lost, smiling incessantly and learning to accept my perceived flaws.
Conduct:	Focus on using dance to elevate my state of mind and position in life. Expressing myself

	freely as an individual and learning to dance in step with partners. Transmuting trauma through body movement and dance.
Personal Disposition:	Evaluating my position in life and learning to respond to the intuitive nudges and lead of the Universe.

On Independence Day of 2017, I moved from Des Moines, Iowa to the Los Angeles, California region. There, dancing took on new meaning as I became more conscious of the influence dance has on my life. Because dancing can be an intimate, individual experience as well as a collective one, I became insistent on learning to dance well with a partner. This learning process required confronting some long-standing patterns, navigating triggers, letting go of control, and setting aside my pride to restart dance as a 48-year-old beginner.

If there's one thing I learned intimately in 2019, it's that we never "arrive." Yes, there's a natural progression to life, but nothing is ever permanent. As much as we heal and advance our lives, there will always be change, loss, gain, and greater learning. While I've come quite far in my TransenDANCE, I've not yet unlocked my final, desired state where I'm intuitively and reflexively responding to life's changing rhythms with patient anticipation and precise movement. However, I know that with a greater understanding of the lessons I'm presenting in this book, that my desired state will be achieved at the perfect time—not a moment too soon and not a moment too late.

TranscenDANCE - Led, Supported, and Thriving	
Time:	Future desired state
Location:	All over the world
Atmosphere:	Moving freely based on the lead of the Universe. Leveraging dance themes to connect with, rely on, and trust in ever-present Universal support.
Life Stage:	Open and available to the opportunities presented.
Appearance:	Naturally gorgeous and exuding confidence.
Conduct:	Moving freely and intuitively while responding to the lead of amazing dance partners. Rising above and going beyond personal expectations, limiting beliefs, and disparaging patterns through dance.
Personal Disposition:	Intuitive, connected, happy, and unfuckwithable.

In the desired state of TransenDANCE, my personal stance, sense of worth, and truth are solid. I connect with dance partners from a place of individual wholeness. We move together fluidly and separate effortlessly when the time comes. My intuition is integrated, trusted, and followed. I'm open to and responsive to the lead of the Universe. It's a forever dance that's expansive, expressive, and filled with love.

TranscenDANCE	
Be and express your whole self; and accept every part of your story—especially the chapters you wish you could hide.	
TranscenDANCE statement:	Life and healing are nonlinear, progressive, and ever-changing. TranscenDANCE is a desired state of being where we are responding to life's challenges with fluidity, intuition, and patience.
TranscenDANCE prompt:	Define and describe your desired state of TranscenDANCE. Spend 30 minutes writing about life where you're led, supported, and thriving. What is taking place? Who is around you? Describe your transformation in detail. For the next 15 minutes, identify and obstacles in the way of achieving TrascenDANCE.
TranscenDANCE Spotify playlist:	**Levels** bit.ly/LevelsPlaylist Life is a journey and we will travel through many layers and levels. Celebrate them all.

If you look at a dancer in silence,
his or her body will be the music.
If you turn the music on, that
body will become an extension of
what you're hearing.
—Judith Jamison

TranscenDANCE

Chapter 3

Express Yourself

At its most basic meaning, dance is about individual expression. Whether dancing alone, with a partner, or in a community, it's our individual expression that contributes to the whole. Dance is art. While many people express in multiple ways—by speaking, writing, painting, singing, acting, exercise, cooking, loving, and caring, **art brings expression to life**. At the same time, **the expression through art gives us life**.

I spent most of my life understanding I was depressed. I say "understanding" rather than "being" because the idea of depression wasn't a knowing that came from within me—except to feel that I didn't fit in. Instead, the depression felt like more of an external mandate that came from other people. Family members, friends, bosses, and doctors repeatedly reminded me, directly or indirectly, that I was different. The word "crazy" was thrown around frequently. After much searching, the feeling of not fitting in was labeled as depression. Starting in 1990, I visited a psychiatrist for the first time, and was clinically diagnosed and heavily medicated for a number of mental health disorders including ADHD, major depressive disorder, anxiety, and even bipolar II. While I was severely depressed and often suicidal throughout my teenage years, it wasn't until I secured my own insurance through full-time employment that I was able to see a therapist. My parents were from the generation that thought therapy was for "crazy people" and there was a significant amount of shame attached to the act of "needing" therapy. At the time, I was a customer service representative for a third-party insurance administrator. I spoke to parents all day long about their children's therapy appointments. I do recall feeling both judgmental of their need for therapy (based on my conditioning) and jealous of their ability to go to therapy (based on their conditioning). Eventually, I decided I could take matters into my own hands to schedule and pay for my own therapy appointments—no parents needed.

I was heavily medicated for over 20 years—at one point taking nearly 1,000 pills every month (including five *different* drugs for mental illness). I took stimulants and anti-depressants to get going in the morning, and benzos, mood stabilizers, and anti-psychotic meds to sleep at night. I once asked my psychiatrist about this really unhealthy pattern, and the need to up my dosage as I built up tolerance levels over time. He basically told me "that's just the way it goes," and I should get used to it because I would spend the rest of my life taking meds to deal with my mental conditions. I fully accepted his assertion and planned for a life chasing woke and begging sleep.

The Universe had other plans. A shrill alarm bell came in the form of a critical illness that caused me to rethink everything, especially counting on a lifetime of medicating my depression.

Shortly before I was "awakened" by critical illness, I joined Facebook, which was life changing for me. While many declare the negative aspects of social media, it continues to be the single most important contributor to my initial and ongoing recovery. Exploring Facebook replaced the murder mystery TV shows I was drawn to. While lying in my bed, I did a ton of reading and research on Facebook and the innerwebs. Through this discovery process, I surmised I really wasn't depressed. I was a suppressed and repressed middle-aged, highly-sensitive person and empath. These were terms I'd never heard before, yet they described me to a T.

According to *Psychology Today*, High Sensitivity is defined as "acute physical, mental, and emotional responses to external (social, environmental) or internal (intra-personal) stimuli."[1] Highly Sensitive People (HSPs) are extremely sensitive to sights, sounds, and the way things feel.

I was the kid who refused to wear polyester clothing because I couldn't stand the way it felt next to my skin. Once at day care, I wet my pants and didn't have anything to change into. The teachers gave me a pair of polyester pants to wear. When my mom picked me up several hours later, the teachers exclaimed, "We have no idea why she's crying. She's been crying all day." My mom took one look at me and said, "It's the polyester." She promptly took me home, bathed me, and gave me fresh, cotton PJs. I finally stopped crying.

I can hear sound from miles away (which is one of the reasons apartment living is challenging for me). My sense of smell is out of this world—which didn't work out so well for my pot-smoking son or alcoholic former boyfriend. The strangest sensitivity I have is to paper. Touching straw wrappers, newspapers, egg cartons, and cardboard boxes creates a similar response from my system like one would experience from hearing fingernails on a chalkboard. Touching these things, or hearing others touch them, like the sound of someone playing with their straw wrapper, makes my skin crawl. Nearly 50 years ago, this level of sensitivity was just plain **weird**. It wasn't understood or talked about; except to shame the "dramatics" of it.

On top of being an HSP, I'm also an empath. Dr. Judith Orloff describes empaths as people who take the experience of an HSP much further by sensing and sometimes absorbing the energy of other people into their own bodies. She expands this noting: "This capacity allows us to experience the energy around us, including emotions and physical sensations, in extremely deep ways. And so we energetically internalize the feelings and pain of others—and often have trouble distinguishing someone else's discomfort from our own."[2]

As an empath who frequently spends time around others, I've been known to experience sudden bursts of anger, sadness, lethargy, and confusion that come out of nowhere. I've been known to get crushing headaches while shopping, or come home utterly exhausted after short excursions. Not knowing anything about being an empath or the embodiment of others' emotions, I owned every emotion as if it were my own for years.

In an attempt to make sense of my world, I started meeting with Intuitive Counselor Rita Henry in 2013. One of the first things she told me was, "This depression, it's not yours." I had no idea what she was talking about. She asserted that I had serially taken on the emotions of other people, particularly my mother. At this time, I had no idea what an empath was or that I was one of them.

Now, I know *and* I'm still not great at not taking on the emotions of other people! But I'm learning new skills and techniques to help with this every day.

After learning more about how I'm made, I understood my body was blowing up—literally and figuratively—because I denied who I was most of my life. I was consistently shut down when I showed any emotion and was constantly told I was "too sensitive." I was led to believe expressing emotion was "crazy" and "unprofessional," yet I frequently had emotional outbursts. There were many times in my work history where I had to leave meetings, or leave the office, because I either couldn't keep my emotions in check or they were unwelcome in the setting. In anticipation of a potential emotional response from me, my CEO boss once told me, "If you're sensitive that day, do something so you won't be sensitive."

In recovery—through coaching, therapy, and intuitive work—I learned to better control my emotions and rarely had outbursts of any kind. I also came to understand that these emotions are signs of LIFE. As a depressed person, I suppressed emotion in favor of numbness, because I fit in better that way. Therapy helped me understand there's nothing inherently wrong with emotion. I remember one time I had a minor disagreement with my boyfriend. I was completely joking, but I really gave him hell. I went off, portraying emotional extremes. His response surprised me and gave me a brand-new perspective. He said, "Good! I'm so glad to see you showing emotion." Say what? For someone who'd been regularly shut down for showing emotion, it was beautiful to be rewarded for it—even when I was joking. This was a completely opposite reaction than what I was used to.

I later understood the value of appropriately expressing emotion. Our truth is often emotional. When you watch a Hallmark movie and cry, that's your truth and resonance with love. I used to get angry when I watched sappy movies. That was my truth at that time. I wasn't a vibrational match to love then, so the sight of it, even in a movie, filled me with anger.

Thankfully, I found a cure or, at least, a means for managing my emotional discourse. Dancing was the medicine that healed me. Expressing myself through dance enabled me to dispel the excess energy, share my emotional truths, tap into my creativity, and connect with others.

In *The Power of Now*, Eckhart Tolle talks about the important spiritual lessons he learned from ducks. He describes the way the ducks float peacefully and at ease with themselves and each other. He also noted that sometimes the ducks would have a spat—usually when one would enter the space of another. What happens after the spat is important: the ducks would go their separate ways and "vigorously flap their wings a few times" before returning to their more-peaceful state. Tolle observed that "by flapping their wings, they were releasing surplus energy, thus preventing it from becoming trapped in their body and turning into negativity. This is natural wisdom, and it is easy for them because they do not have a mind that keeps the past alive unnecessarily and then builds an identity around it." Boys on the playground often do the same thing. They'll resolve problems through fistfights and then quickly go back to being friends.

Dancing afforded me better health while enabling me to do the same thing ducks and young boys do. Flapping my wings—dancing—allows me to release the pent-up, potentially harmful energy that builds because I'm an HSP and an empath with a mind often doing laps of overthinking.

Obsessing, ruminating, and overthinking is the opposite of more healthful expressions and lead to disease. According to Dr. Bradley Nelson in *The Emotion Code*, "Trapped emotions are perhaps the most common type of imbalance that human beings suffer from. [All] trapped emotions can be implicated in nearly all diseases, either directly or indirectly." It's no wonder I got so sick. My body was full with a lifetime of suppressed and repressed emotion. It's no wonder dance is so healing; symptoms return when I don't dance. To be clear, when I'm talking about dance, I'm talking about simply moving your body rhythmically to some music. I'm not talking about specific dance routines, styles, or genres; and I'm not talking about being a stellar dancer. I'm not one, but I'm invested in moving through the Universe via dance for my health and well-being.

The same effects of moving emotions from your body can be accomplished through any movement; whether that's walking, yoga, CrossFit, or any other modality. I just happen to smile and enjoy myself more when I'm dancing. If CrossFit makes you smile incessantly, go for it!

[1] https://www.psychologytoday.com/us/blog/communication-success/201711/24-signs-highly-sensitive-person

[2] https://www.psychologytoday.com/us/blog/the-empaths-survival-guide/201706/the-differences-between-highly-sensitive-people-and-empaths

TranscenDANCE	
Accept your sensitivity as the gift that it is.	
TranscenDANCE statement:	Expressing through art, dance, writing and other means allows us to expel excess energy, connect to our truth, and stay in touch with the person we really are.
TranscenDANCE prompt:	Paint or draw your truth. Use creativity to visually represent who you are and the truth of your desires. Your masterpiece should represent the essence of who you truly are.
TranscenDANCE Spotify playlist:	**Good Morning** bit.ly/GoodMorningPlaylist This playlist is filled with songs about having a good life. Don't leave your mornings to chance. Start your day off with positivity, hope, and encouragement.

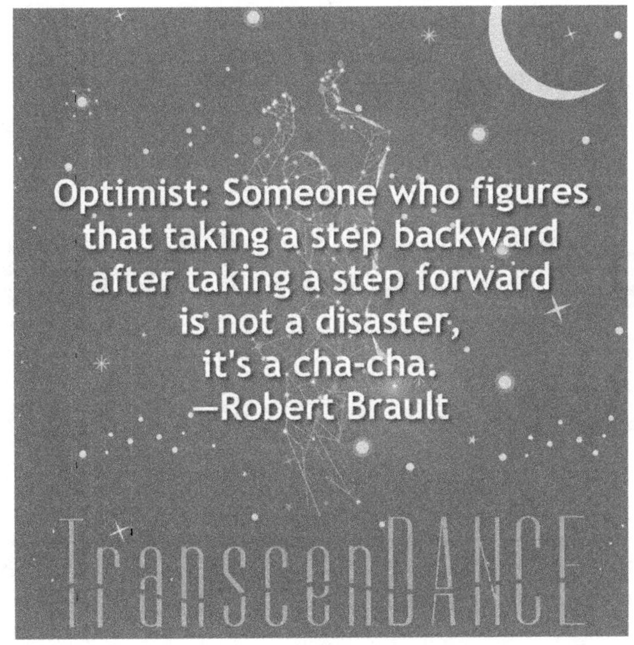
Optimist: Someone who figures
that taking a step backward
after taking a step forward
is not a disaster,
it's a cha-cha.
—Robert Brault
TranscenDANCE

Chapter 4

The Pivot and the Pause

Life—and healing especially—isn't a straight line. I've come to a place in recovery where I'm tired. As often as I want to throw in the towel, I know living, recovering, and accessing higher levels of consciousness is worth it. At the same time, the awakened life isn't for the faint of heart. Healing is sometimes exhausting; it's also messy. It's arduous, painful, and relentless. When we think we're solving one problem, we often find more to solve—or come to find out that the problem we thought we solved, has resurfaced in a new way—sometimes repeatedly and with vengeance.

While many think of recovery in terms of stopping an addiction, it's my belief that everyone is recovering from something—which may very well be an addiction, but not necessarily in the traditional sense of one who is addicted to alcohol or drugs. I wasn't addicted to one substance over another.

Rather, I have addictive behaviors and tendencies toward numbing rather than acknowledging and processing my own feelings. I was frequently distracted, and often searched for things outside of myself to make me feel whole and complete.

I'm recovering from many things: among them are depression, suicidal ideation, trauma, neglect, critical illness, and more traditional addictions with substances, food, and sex. The more I learn about recovery, the more I understand the things we often blame as catalysts for recovery in the first place—like a traumatic childhood, a narcissistic lover, and feeling unloved—are often exacerbated by our internal state of mind. More accurately-stated, we can get lost in our perception of a circumstance, without taking the time to heal and understand the reality of it. When that happens, it's nearly impossible to take responsibility for the ways we contributed to the problem(s) and do the work to heal matters of the heart, mind, and soul.

Taking personal responsibility and staying committed to self-improvement is not easy—especially once I realized I'm my own biggest challenge. However, that doesn't make it any less important or worthwhile. Two concepts from dance that I revisit frequently during my own recovery journey are the pivot and the pause.

A pivot is defined as a "turn or twist." You'll hear later about my obsessions with fancy turns. For now, know that a pivot to me is a sometimes-subtle movement used to change your trajectory. When we're evaluating our environment and not getting the results we desire, a pivot is used to change things up. We do this in business all the time. Growing up in direct mail (yes, back in the day before email and the internet) pivots were the name of the game to score better results from direct mail offers. Our team obsessively analyzed data and made sometimes miniscule adjustments like changing the envelope color, choosing a different return address, or using a slightly different copy variation. Each test was measured against a control package to see which one performed the best. Once new packages were deemed "winners" by achieving a greater response rate, we never stopped testing. The new winner became the control package, and all new variations were tested against the new winner.

I believe that's what we should do in life. Even when things are working and going well, there's always room for improvement. We should consistently be evaluating ways to make incremental improvements and find new "winning" strategies.

While the pivot comes naturally for me, the pause has been a bit more challenging. Recently, in dance class while I was learning a new move, I could not stay with my partner. As we broke down the steps, we realized I was moving through the pause, which totally threw things off. That particular sequence required a short pause before the finish and my failure to heed the pause made it challenging for me to stay in sync with my partner.

My failure to take a proper pause in life caused similar challenges. What is a proper pause? For me, it's resting without guilt, getting enough sleep, taking care of my personal life and business while also making space for fun. It seems most of us were conditioned to continue moving forward at all costs—particularly in the entrepreneurial space. There's glory in "the hustle." Only it's my belief that hustling comes from a place of lack.

Everyone is hustling for their dreams, but are they really? I now believe hustle kills dreams. Hustle is not the same as working harder, or more importantly, working smarter. Work is always required to make your dreams come true. But you know what else is required? Relaxation, self-care, stillness, downtime, and **joy** as an integral part of the equation. These gifts are often found while dancing, meditating, connecting with others, and just BEing ourselves.

Hustle wakes me up in the middle of the night to work. Hustle keeps me up all night and avoiding my body's need for sleep. Hustle keeps me at the computer on social media while friends and family are standing by—longing for company. Hustle keeps me meeting the needs of others while my own needs fall by the wayside. Hustling has me multitasking at a rate that defies comprehension. Hustling worries whether or not the payments will come through in time. Hustling often means people-pleasing. Full stop.

Hustling comes from a place of lack. Hustling is rooted in the belief that we must get ours before it runs out. Hustling represents a lack of trust. Stopping the hustle subscribes to a position of abundance, strength, and worth. Stopping the hustle demonstrates commitment, courage, and determination. Stopping the hustle requires owning your power and using it ways that add value while balancing it with **life**. Stopping the hustle requires establishment of systems, processes, and networks of people to serve yourself and others. Stopping the hustle begins with a commitment to who you are and protecting that valuable asset at all costs.

For me, I think the fear of pausing comes back to a fear that I will stop. I don't ever want to go back to my depressed days where I couldn't get out of bed and while failing to claim my own worth over the worth of others. My dance instructor, Stephen balances the dance pause beautifully, stating:

> When we pause in dancing, we never actually stop completely. We change the energy to slow down and almost come to a complete stop, but we keep a slight movement as we continue the weight transfer and slow down the reaction through the body. With the slightest bit of movement still alive in the body, and hardly noticeable to the eye, it enables us to move fluidly into the next step or movement without losing rhythm or losing the beat. We are magicians employing many tools and tricks including variable speed to create dynamics and illusions.

The message is clear: a pause is a dynamic, yet slower movement that creates a more fluid overall experience. Pausing doesn't mean working on your job until you're abruptly forced to stop because of illness; instead it's simply acknowledging a necessary energy change. Not only is our purpose alive and well, it will bounce back higher and with more intent after an effective pause.

TranscenDANCE	
Pause to take a break. **Pivot so you can travel in new directions.**	
TranscenDANCE statement:	Pausing is a slow dynamic movement for rest and rejuvenation. Pivoting is a subtle movement that allows us to re-evaluate our environment and make changes. Both are vital for an awakened life.
TranscenDANCE prompt:	Make your own detour! Pivot by taking a new route to a routine place like work, the gym, or the grocery store. Did you notice anything special on the new route? How did you feel doing something new?
TranscenDANCE Spotify playlist:	**In Da Feels** bit.ly/InDaFeelsPlaylist This is the saddest playlist ever! There's no fake positivity here. When you need to cry and feel da feels, listen to this playlist and pause to grieve before pivoting.

To dance is to be
out of yourself.
Larger, more beautiful,
more powerful...
This is power,
it is glory on earth and
it is yours for the taking.
—Agnes De Mille

TranscenDANCE

Chapter 5

Dance and other "Medicine"

Who doesn't want to be richer in spirit, more beautiful, and more powerful? So many of us spend our lives playing so small, it's hard to imagine being and accepting the glory in the Universe that's ours for the taking. We concentrate on our weaknesses, fail to accept our imperfections, and ignore our gifts in the name of being "safe," as in, free from fear. Marianne Williamson's famous quote reminds us to accept our birthright to be all we can be:

> Our greatest fear is not that we are inadequate. Our deepest fear is that we are powerful beyond measure. It is our light, not our darkness that most frightens us. We ask ourselves, Who am I to be brilliant, gorgeous, talented, fabulous? Actually, who are you not to be? Your playing small does not serve the world. We were born to make

manifest the glory of God that is within us. And as we let our own light shine, we unconsciously give other people permission to do the same.

When I dance, I find glimpses of glory on the dance floor. They may be fleeting, they may vary from song to song, dance to dance, but they're there. Their appearance revealed to me I wasn't alone in life and needn't resist life's rhythms. Dancing was the medicine I needed to heal a lifetime of depression—one Friday night at a time.

I didn't know why, but I knew I needed to dance. By the time Friday rolled around, I made my way to the dance floor at Denny Arthur's Dance Club in Urbandale, Iowa. Denny, the bar owner, established the place in April of 1980 as an "Over 30" dance club. It was the only club of its kind and it stood the test of time, gaining in popularity with every passing decade while other clubs opened and closed quickly. The patrons at Denny's were as varied as customers at Walmart or citizens at the state fair—which in Iowa, is quite fun for people-watching. Free Spin: The people watching at the California State Fair isn't nearly as fun as it is at the Iowa State Fair. I'm not sure I even saw a single mullet. I certainly didn't see oversized guts or titties hanging out.

At Denny Arthur's, the average age on the dance floor at 8 pm was unusually high but decreased by the hour as the night progressed. In my earlier dance days, I was known to call the club "Arthur's over 80." In my later years, I arrived early just to see the 80-year-old couples strut their stuff with the most eloquent partner dances. I longed to move like them—at any age, but especially at such advanced ages. After midnight, the bar transformed into a college party with the kids pursuing the quirky goodness that is Denny's and the usual closing time shenanigans appeared.

Under the disco ball, I left behind my anxiety, the stressors of the week, the build-up of nervous energy, crushing responsibilities, and loneliness. I traded overwhelm for creative expression, joy, and boundless, uninhibited smiles. Free Spin: My son's best friend Collin who grew up at our house lived with me at the time. He was accustomed to me spending all of my time in bed. I can't tell you how many times he called me to check up on me and make sure I was ok when he'd arrive at the house and I wasn't home. Also, I frequently referred to the club as Denny's. It took him several months before he figured out I was at a dance club, not the breakfast place.

Although I enjoyed the healing effects I received from dance, it wasn't until much later that I made the connection between dancing and the therapeutic results I would experience. I've always had a problem being "in my body." I'd spent most of my life suppressing and repressing my needs in a way that completely blocked my ability to feel safe in my own skin and trust messages from my body. My inability to heed my body's simplest messages about hunger and satiation was easily evidenced by excessive weight gain. While I was always a healthy, thin child and young adult, I began putting on massive amounts of weight starting around age 20.

With the knowledge I've acquired over the last few years regarding my lack of self-expression, I recognize and understand the pattern. I started gaining weight shortly after I began dating my husband. I met him in June of 1991. He had lived in Des Moines, but was attending college out of state. I fully expected we'd have a summer fling and he'd head back to school. In early August, as I was expecting the relationship to come to an end, he chose not to leave. When he told me his plans changed, I exclaimed, "What do you mean you're not going back? You have to go back."

After another month or two went by, I tried to break up with him. He cried. I'd never seen a man cry. Even though I knew in my heart that this man wasn't my true love, I knew nothing but co-dependent love. In turn, I swallowed my resolve, repressed my honest desires, and suppressed my own needs in an effort to comfort him and do what I thought was the "right thing." Instead of standing in and speaking my truth, I felt an increasing need to numb the uncomfortable feelings that arose from the failure to do so. I've repeated this pattern countless times since. This is one of the lessons that continues to resurface for me. Thankfully, I'm much closer to my own truth these days and am better at expressing it. At the same time, I stand firmly in my belief that everything happens for a reason. Had I not stayed with my husband, we wouldn't have married, and we wouldn't have had our son Johnathan, who is the greatest gift I know.

Thea Elijah from the publication *WhiteAwake* explains why being in our body is important:

> Our body speaks to us all the time. For instance, it tells us when we are hungry, or when we are tired. If we are not fully in our body, though, we may not notice these signals until they get very loud and obvious. The more we are in our body, the more our body can whisper to us, instead of having to shout. When we are fully in our body, our bodies can whisper to us about many more things than just hunger or tiredness. Our bodies become increasingly able to inform

> us about other needs, feelings, inspirations and intuitions from within us. We also become increasingly able to hear what our bodies are sensing around us, in our environment, much as animals and children often seem to have a "sixth sense" about what is going on around them. When we know how to listen to the whispers of our body, our bodies can be a means by which we tune in to a very subtle level of perception that is natural to all of us.[1]

You've likely heard the quote from Oprah about listening to the whispers: "Difficulties come when you don't pay attention to life's whisper. Life always whispers to you first, but if you ignore the whisper, sooner or later you'll get a scream." When I supressed and denied who I am, when any of us does, the body has no choice but to scream for attention. And boy, did my body scream!

It happened the day after my son left for an out-of-state trade school in August of 2014. I was not your typical empty nest mom who couldn't imagine being in the house without my son. Instead, I welcomed the change. As a single mom since my son was two years old, he and I have always been extremely close. However, we had an extraordinarily tough senior year complete with drug use, multiple arrests, and mental health struggles. I've never been arrested, but my son wasn't the only one with drug use and mental health struggles. By the time he graduated high school, I was ready for my son to get outta dodge, and he urgently needed a fresh start.

My mental health was precarious, and was exacerbated by the ridiculous amount of prescriptions I took, including narcotic pain killers. I wasn't just trying to drown out the disruption in my mind, I frequently tried to escape the reality and the crushing demands of a being single parent. Escape through numbing took me away from being the emotionally-available parent I desired to be. I grew up essentially without parents. They were married and home for the most part, but they weren't available to me. We never communicated or spent time together, each doing our own things and feeling desperately alone at the same time. Through coaching, I realized the emotional unavailability of my parents—and later, the romantic partners I chose—is one of my biggest childhood wounds. I was ashamed to recognize that I repeated this pattern with my own son. Starting around the time my mother died, and a couple of years into my seven-year stint in bed, I was prescribed a narcotic nasal spray for migraine headaches. This spray would not only knock out a migraine in an instant, it knocked me out too. I loved the feeling of being dead to the world. I clung to prescription refills for the high that brought me to the lowest low. When my enabler (I mean doctor) retired in 2013 and I could no longer get refills, I quit cold turkey. Looking back, it's no wonder my son struggled so much. It's hard for a developing child to stay on track with an unavailable parent drowning in depression, using, and spending all her time in bed.

Years later, just as I was looking forward to concentrating on myself in my newly-created empty nest, I became chronically ill with a hostile digestive disease and unrelated menstrual complications. My body let me know in no uncertain terms that when I was not my authentic self, when I resisted the flow of the Universe, I was full of shit. I'm being literal here; the process of physically excreting all that I psychically, emotionally, and spiritually backed up was most inconvenient. This is no exaggeration: I let go of so much shit, I lost 110 pounds in nine months from this illness.

Interestingly, being ill fueled my need to dance even more. It was as if I intuited the release as foretelling the process of getting aligned with the Universe. Often, our group of Smart Wild Kinky Mamas would go out to dinner before dancing. I'd eat, get sick in short fashion, and head to dance. Something on the dance floor pulled me. The joy and freedom I felt when moving my body couldn't be overshadowed by my dramatic bodily reaction. I may've been nauseated before each next session, but the electric energy of the dance floor rallied me, and I couldn't stop smiling when I was in my element of dance.

My smile was a bit conspicuous though—especially because I was often sick. The truth is, my smile was mostly an involuntary reaction. I couldn't not smile when I was dancing. Though I was smiling, my body was undergoing significant deterioration combatting two concurrent chronic illnesses. Free Spin: Speaking of conspicuous smiles. One day, I was walking through the office at my most stressful job with the biggest smile on my face. A co-worker gave me a puzzled look. I announced, "I'm smiling because I took my tranquilizers at lunch." If I knew then what I know now, I'd choose to have a dance break instead.

And there was certainly a transitional period as I got used to the idea of freeing myself via dance. Consciously, I was ready to embrace the spiritual liberation dance was affording me. Unconsciously, there was much more resistance. At first, as I delved into dance, I utilized "liquid courage" to fit in with the crowd and be freer in my movement. I didn't return to my bingeing days but I was drinking more than I had in years which, in turn, didn't help my digestive or menstrual issues. I also hadn't gotten any younger in a decade, so my sometimes-hangovers lasted far longer than they used to.

When my digestive disease required me to be alcohol-free during a 14-day treatment, I tried something new. I couldn't imagine not dancing for those two weeks, so I danced without drinking. Guess what? I survived. Even better, I saved money on drinks and Uber rides, drove home safely, and woke up clear. While it did take a bit more courage to dance freely without the lubricant of alcohol, I actually loved being sober on the dance floor even more. I could see and feel everything and I didn't have to question intentions, especially my own. Most importantly, I stepped on fewer toes and could keep up with partners. Getting more conscious and coming out the other side of my emotional and bodily battles helped me become even more present and more open to the Universe as dance instructor.

What I know now is that being in my body is essential to tap into intuitive gifts. And dancing is intrinsically about being in my body. It's a very grounding experience for me. Once I started releasing energy, ego, reluctance, and insecurity via dance, my body started to respond; it began a mental, physical, and emotional cleansing.

[1]https://whiteawake.org/what-does-it-mean-to-be-in-your-body/

TranscenDANCE	
Tune into and respect your body's "Yes."	
TranscenDANCE statement:	It is natural to turn to "medicines" to ease discomfort. However, the "medicine" may express itself as a coping mechanism. Effective coping mechanisms are healthy and aligned with our highest good. However, often the patterns we turn to most frequently are not healthy or aligned. Connect with your body to determine if the coping mechanisms are beneficial or detrimental.
TranscenDANCE prompt:	Write down your coping mechanisms. Be honest: is it food, shopping, substances, porn? Are these mechanisms in alignment with your highest self? If not, consider new coping mechanisms and challenge yourself to use them. For example, when feeling sluggish and wanting to eat, step outside for a short walk instead.

TranscenDANCE Spotify playlist:	**Addictions** bit.ly/AddictionsPlaylist This playlist is full of music with lyrics associated with addictions. For me, it's a reminder of what I miss out on when I use unhealthy coping mechanisms.

Dance mates are the
new soul mates.
—Vanessa Sandberg
TranscenDANCE

Chapter 6

My Truth about Dance and Life Partners

I laugh when I think about my evolution of dance partners, or any other partners, for that matter. I remember going to a Valentine's Day singles' dance after my divorce. I felt obligated to say "yes" to literally anyone and everyone who asked me to dance—even if I wasn't the least bit attracted to them, or didn't feel like dancing, or didn't like the song. My good friend Sue once asked me why I did that. She's always been good at challenging me to evolve my thinking. My honest reply was, "I didn't realize I had a choice." The emotion below my instinctive reply to Sue was a mixture of feeling glad to be asked, feeling sorry for the men who asked, *and* having no idea how to say "No" in a way that didn't hurt them or make me feel shitty about saying no. This is a big deal; I got married for the same reason. In all cases, my response was about the other person, never about my own feelings, even when my body sent me alarm bells and warnings.

What I know now—after decades of therapy and coaching—is the importance of recognizing, standing in, and staying true to my needs and desires. It's the most loving thing I can do for me *and everyone I interact with*. While it may not always be agreeable to others, expressing my truth with integrity and love is, for me, never a bad idea. In the last nine months, I've literally taken this concept so far that I've walked out in the middle of a first date and asked a partner to leave my house in the middle of the night when it became clear that we were not a good match. Free Spin: I love the movie *When Harry Met Sally*. I often think of the New Year's Eve scene when Harry exclaims to Sally, "When you realize you want to spend the rest of your life with someone, you want the rest of your life to start now." In 2019, it became clear to me that the reverse is also true: If you're certain you don't want to spend the rest of your life with someone, you want the rest of your life to start now.

I didn't always have the clarity and courage to take care of myself first. And, I certainly wasn't strong enough in my own stance to commit to it. In terms of partners, I have a tendency to immediately attach to a new partner (however fleeting the encounter may have been) and make the rendezvous mean something. I remember the first time I did this like it was yesterday. I was a freshman in high school and a wrestling mat maid. I made out with a wrestler, a very popular junior boy, at a party over the weekend. By Monday, I was bragging on the bus about how I was "going out" with the boy I locked lips with. I was shocked to find out he had a girlfriend and that "making out" didn't equal "going out."

In addition to immediately attaching to partners, I've been known to indiscriminately give them my all—usually to my own detriment. Often, this includes taking responsibility for their happiness, while subconsciously giving them responsibility for mine. Now, I'm becoming more discerning and being more careful to recognize a date is just a date, not a relationship. Especially on the dance floor, a dance is just a dance. There's absolutely nothing wrong with dating, dancing with, and getting to know potential partners in order to determine the very best match before becoming true partners and making an exclusive commitment.

In the same way I desire partners to respect my truth, it's important for me to respect theirs. My problem has always been a tendency toward self-deprecation. When relationships don't work out—dancing, dating, or otherwise—my instinct is to question what I did wrong and figure out how I can fix **me** in order to make things work, not realizing that not everything is meant to work. And maybe, just maybe, I'm not the one with the problem. Even better, it's possible for things not to work out simply because they don't, not because there's any problem whatsoever. Sometimes partners just want different things, have different values, and show up differently in the world; and that's okay. There's no problem to solve and nothing to fix. In that case, there's simply a lack of alignment, and there's no need to project a negative light on either partner.

I think the most important aspect of this perspective is being a person with a strong enough center, that is moral code, sense of integrity, and recognition of self-worth. When I have a strong center, then relationship failures don't knock me so far off balance and cause me to go into the questioning mode I'm accustomed to. A group dance instructor named Roy recently put the idea of "fault" into perspective for me when he said, "Let's try that with a new partner. If it didn't work, maybe it wasn't you." I've literally had advanced dance partners ditch me mid-dance because they've said I'm not a good follower. These dancers know damn well they're a good lead and they don't second guess themselves for a moment. In other words, they aren't knocked off their own center when things don't work out on the dance floor. They know I'm the problem. As someone who grew up on the "It's not you, it's me," phenomenon for too long, I got used to accepting responsibility for shortcomings—even when they weren't mine to accept.

When Roy suggested trying things with a new partner, he was essentially saying, "Don't assume you're bad at this if it doesn't go well or as expected. It may not be a good fit." This was a reminder that it's personally harmful to immediately surmise I am the one causing a problem. Instead, it's an invitation to keep dancing rather than jumping into a trauma pattern of self-blame.

I've spent too much of my life settling for less than the "full package" when it comes to connection and partnership. I've rearranged my thoughts, my plans, and my life to accommodate partners with minimal connections. Free Spin: "Back in the day," one of my friends was casually dating a man who needed a washer and dryer. I honestly considered selling my own washer and dryer because I was sure I'd be moving in with a new man I met on the internet and wouldn't need them anymore. Our consistent ongoing joke among friends when we'd get in over our heads was, "Don't sell the washer and dryer!" This phrase lended instant focus when any of us would get ahead of ourselves.

I rationalized those choices with unhealthy self-talk like, "But the sex is so good (and he doesn't listen to me)," or "He asked (and I didn't have the heart to say no)," or "He's so respectful and generous (except in the bedroom)," or "He has a beautiful spirit (and no job)," or "He really sees and understands me (and lives out of state)," or "He's here now (and his wife doesn't know)," or "He's the best communicator I've ever talked to (and he doesn't accept all of me)." Remember how much I love duality? To be honest, I've found it hard to embody the fact that I'm deserving of the full package in spite of my perceived imperfections. My lack of self-acceptance and my inability to remain centered have often caused me to attract and commit to others who had similar issues, sometimes resulting in trauma-bonding. This quote from Abraham Hicks is really deep, but it sums this up perfectly:

> A lot of times you are a vibrational match for the very thing you do not want. Because you're afraid you won't get what you want and so you're a vibrational match to the absence of what you want. And then, the absence of what you want walks in and you think, "Oh, that must surely be it, because it feels like a match." [It feels like a match] because it **is** a match, but it's not a match to what you want, it's a match to where you **are.**

I recognized recently that my history of accepting less-than-stellar partners came from a place of lack and is the result of scarcity thinking. I've been operating from a place of, "It's better to have something—even something bad—than to have nothing at all." At the same time, I'm looking for others to fill a void I haven't filled myself. Of course, the result is a string of either unavailable partners or ones with minimal connection points; of noncommittal dudes with an inability to join me in my elaborate dance of life. My incomplete healing and dysfunctional patterns invited friends-with-benefits arrangements, a lackluster love life, and intense longing for something more expansive.

When it comes to dancing—or dating, or relationships—a better stance is one where I fully own my worth, my integrity, and my love as the incredibly valuable asset it is. When a personal situation doesn't work out, it doesn't have to be a reflection of me and my worth. Instead, it can just be a partner standing in his own truth that's different from mine. It took me a long time to get to the point where I understood the concept of facing an opposing view and not taking personal offense or getting defensive. What I know now is that it's important to simply stand in my truth while allowing others to do the same.

A recent break-up ended with me saying "I'm really sorry." He responded with, "Yes, me too, beautiful. But nothing for you to be sorry about." Wow! I'm 48-years-old and that's a perspective I've never considered. I sincerely thanked him for the lesson and the awareness—knowing full well that his compassion toward me was a reflection of the self-compassion I worked hard to gain through this healing and recovery process.

TranscenDANCE	
Accept dances, friendships, and lovers without leaping immediately to attach to them.	
TranscenDANCE statement:	Standing in our truth often means understanding we are in charge of our choices and of exercising discernment. This requires trust in our decisions, our worth, and our faith.
TranscenDANCE prompt:	A way to manifest love is through a love ritual. Draw a bath with the following elements: flowers (roses, lilac, jasmine), crystals or other stones (rose quartz, tourmaline, rhodonite, jade), and pink Himalayan salt. Close your eyes and meditate on the love, romance and passion you are calling in, for 10-15 minutes.
TranscenDANCE Spotify playlist:	**Manifesting Love** bit.ly/ManifestingLovePlaylist Love is exciting and fun. This playlist is full of love songs to get you thinking about your "fuck yes and nothing less" love.

This is why the idea of
finding love across the
dance floor endures
- symbolizing that, when we
know the true rhythm
of our heart,
we know the other.
—Alexandra Katehakis

TranscenDANCE

Chapter 7

Leading and Following

There's magic in being led well on the dance floor.

It was the late 80s at the Stillwell Junior High Sadie Hawkins Valentine's Day dance. My date, surprisingly adept for a barely-teenaged boy, said to me, "I'll lead." I wasn't sure what he meant by that exactly, but I suspected he took dance lessons because the words "I'll lead" don't commonly fall out of 13-year-old boy's mouth. Sure enough, when I ran into that same boy as a grown man 20 years later, my suppositions were confirmed. He confessed he prepared by seeking dance lessons in advance of our big junior high date.

While I was too young to appreciate my date leading me at the junior high dance, I definitely experienced what's truly meant by being well-led by a partner during my dance renaissance in Southern California years after seeing that grown-up boy.

After my son left for college, I stumbled across an article by blogger Matthew Fray. It's an excellent discussion of relationships. In the article Fray states, "The sexiest thing a man can say to his partner is 'I got this,' and then take care of whatever needs taken care of."[1]

That's what leading is about, right?

Yes; mostly. But there's also more.

Women (particularly stubborn, independent women like me) often have a hard time allowing their partner—or even friends, or family members—to help them. This can be off-putting and even emasculating for some men. This practice of self-sufficiency and taking care of everything also leads to isolation for us women. It creates a constant need to stay hypervigilant and always in control of all aspects of life.

There's a reason why we do this. It's because many of us had to step up and do everything on our own. As a single mother for 22 years, I had no choice but to operate in masculine energy, often just to survive. At a very basic, biological level, when you look at the way our sexes are designed, men are designed to give and women are designed to receive. However, women are placed in roles where they must give—to a sometimes-exhausting point. This may not be healthy, but is sometimes necessary. We must work, pay the bills, put food on the table, and care for our children. The idea of receiving—love, accolades, assistance, and rest—is foreign to us, because we've been so used to doing everything on our own. Allowing a man to give, simply by leading the dance a bit—metaphorically and literally—isn't something that comes easily to women who are self-sufficient and independent.

Allowing a partner to lead is challenging. Generally, I dance alone or with a group of girls. Every now and then, I'm fortunate enough to have a partner to lead me on the dance floor.
At first, when dancing with a partner, I am often attempted to take the lead. It's not purposeful or vain, it just happens because it's not natural for me to **be led** in nearly any area of my life.

Leadership is natural for me, following is not.

I learned to counter my tendency to lead by closing my eyes when dancing with a partner, which enables me to feel and mirror my partner's movements with my body instead of second-guessing dance floor leadership roles with my mind. Closing my eyes disallows me to take over. Admittedly, it looks a little strange and often takes my dance partner a minute to adjust.

After taking seven group salsa lessons, I experienced being led well by a partner. Let me explain. I took my salsa classes alone. Half of the class time was dedicated to independent study. During this time, the instructor walked us through the dance steps and we practiced them as a group, with each person practicing the steps on their own. The other half of the class was dedicated to dancing with others as the lead dancer, usually a man, rotates and changes partners every few minutes. It's like speed dating for dance. In this process, you'd think all the onus is on the man as leader, but being a good following partner takes skill and intuition as well. It requires me, and other strong women like me, to relax a bit, exhibit trust, and have patience. And not only for my leading partner, but so I can better enjoy the dance.

Of the three skills, I've gotten pretty good at trusting myself—I know I can count on me. However, relaxation and patience often elude me.

Once, with a new young partner I'd never met before we were paired, I found myself overturning, overstepping, and tripping over my own feet. I wasn't trusting, I wasn't relaxing, I wasn't patient. At some point, my dance partner took my hand and waist and declared, in a way I'd not experienced before, "It's okay. I've got you."

Those words were a trigger for me and it was as if a switch was flipped, now knowing I was "being held," which enabled me to relax into the situation and find new patience with myself. Suddenly, it didn't matter if I spun a little too hard on my turn, overstepped, or tripped, because my partner had a good enough hold on me—physically, but also emotionally—to make the proper corrections for us. When doing a cross body lead, my partner literally opened up space for me to step into. Although our dancing bond lasted for only 10 minutes or so, the education, the surrendering to the dance, was profound.

I remembered a dance class I took with a lover a few years before. This was the love I claimed as my "twin flame." After time and distance from the relationship, I'm more certain this was a trauma bond than a twin flame. However, at the time, I was convinced we were intimately connected and destined to spend more lifetimes together—especially given the nature of our first meeting, our long-standing respect for one another, and a serendipitous reacquaintance over a decade later. We met at a fundraiser for his young nephew with a very serious heart condition. In the raffle, I purchased a heating and cooling maintenance package. For a few years afterward, the man serviced my heater every fall and my air conditioner every spring. We initially met during my depressed years, even during the time when I was bedridden. I weighed more than 300 pounds. Our relationship was strictly professional as he was married and a committed husband and father.

In 2008, a sewage flood in my basement required all my equipment be replaced. After that, because everything was new, I didn't see the need for regular maintenance calls and failed to renew my service contract. When I saw him across the dance floor at Denny Arthur's in 2015, my heart fluttered. I'd heard from a friend he'd divorced and I'd been waiting to run into him.

I walked up to him with the cheesiest line you could deliver to a heating/cooling guy: "You really should check the temperature on the dance floor." He gave me a blank look, so I asked him if he remembered me, and he still shook his head in puzzlement. "It's Melissa Drake," I exclaimed. His resulting expression was priceless. He gave my body a once-over and blurted out, "Holy shit! You must be really proud of yourself," remarking on my 110-pound weight loss. I replied, "It's not like that, but thank you." I wasn't about to go into the details of the menstrual and intestinal issues I'd suffered.

We danced and started the relationship I believed we were always meant to have. I'm certain we've experienced many lifetimes together as our connection was out of this world in many ways. He was a man who learned to completely trust God for every need. His motto was, "Take life as it comes." He was very spontaneous, planned very little, **and** was abundantly blessed. I, on the other hand, having recently recovered from depression, was deep in my ego, trying to find my way, and constantly trying to control specific outcomes. I was fortunate to have just been released from my 25-year corporate career with a nice severance package that gave me time to really decide what I wanted to do with my life. As blessed as I was, at this point in my life, I wanted more, and I wanted it immediately. Because of this, I pushed for my needs to be met, a big commitment, and extreme togetherness. In other words, I was in my masculine trying to control things.

Dance lessons with this lover were a great experience. But after five classes together, we couldn't move past a stance with measured steps of "slow, slow, quick, quick." In hindsight, I see our lack of advancement was because I didn't allow him to lead. Instead, I tried to. In other words, I failed to surrender. I didn't trust the process.

Being led—once I learned to let myself—feels amazingly beautiful. It requires patience; it requires allowing space to be opened up. And it feels like being with a partner who sets me up to succeed and who has my back, always. Being led means having a partner who clears the path to usher me in. It feels like being held, even when you're doing your own thing. In other words, it feels a lot like love. The person who showed me what being led feels like was the young man at salsa lessons. He was a complete stranger, yet, his lead held me in love. Once I surrendered, I allowed him to lead and dancing was a blast.

The greatest lead dancer in the universe **is** the Universe. The Universe is always availing us opportunities to work things out in our favor so we can succeed. It just depends on if we are trusting enough to allow the Universe to lead us through the dance; if we can avail ourselves to the opportunity being presented. The

Universe clears the path so we can walk into the full authority of our lives. We are always held, led, spun, dipped, lifted by our dance partner, the Universe, even when it sometimes doesn't feel like it. And yeah, the Universe is totally in love with us; so why not let it lead?

[1]https://mustbethistalltoride.com/2016/01/14/she-divorced-me-because-i-left- -by-the-sink/

TranscenDANCE	
Surrender control to someone else's lead.	
TranscenDANCE statement:	Life is a dance between taking the lead and following. Often, we identify and express one or the other. Following requires surrendering, relaxing, and releasing control.
TranscenDANCE prompt:	Try a new experience that requires that you trust in the process. (Get a massage, a new haircut, try a new style of clothing, ask someone to lunch, ask someone to dance, or share something vulnerable with a friend.)
TranscenDANCE Spotify playlist:	**Take My Hand** bit.ly/TakeMyHandPlaylist Trying something new requires a bit of trust. This one song playlist will give you the courage to take the lead of the Universe.

Opportunity dances
with those already on
the dance floor.
—H. Jackson Brown, Jr.
TranscenDANCE

Chapter 8

Collaborative Dance

Brené Brown recently made famous a quote from Theodore Roosevelt about the difference between critics and people "in the arena." Those fighting the good fight are "daring greatly," striving, erring, and coming up short; they just don't quit. I believe people on the dance floor are courageously facing their fears even while looking or feeling slightly foolish. People who dance more healthily ignore their inhibitions and insecurities. I've been to a club where wallflowers are making fun of other people's goofy dance moves. My first thought is, "It's easy to make fun of someone from the side line. At least the dancing person has the balls to be on the floor," that is, "in the arena." There's no question in my mind that the dancer—no matter how unusual their dance skills—is having much more fun than the people making fun of her.

In addition to gossiping wallflowers, there are people who are literally moved by the music, but fail to get out on the floor. They may groove in their chair, bounce amongst their friends standing on the side, or dance in place by the bar, but they never once enjoy time under the disco ball. This saddens me. I think the main reason why people who love to dance fail to dance in a club is they're not comfortable dancing alone and/or they're with people who don't want to dance. I've also known people who are only comfortable dancing with partners of the opposite sex rather than in a group of friends. Instead of breaking away from their pack and from societal norms to dance more actively, they inhibit themselves and sway where they are, never realizing their full dance potential. I'll talk more about the value of dancing alone and with a supportive group in the next chapter, but here I want to tell you about how I came to know collaborative dance and what it means to me.

My parents joined Facebook before I did. I resisted the thing that ultimately saved my life for far too long. I'll be the first to admit Facebook is the reason I'm here today, literally and figuratively. In all honesty, I didn't join Facebook because my boss at the time was a fanatic about it. She was friends with everyone and Facebook posts were the talk of the office. While I was an amazing worker, my home life—and therefore my potential Facebook posts—were a mess. I didn't want my coworkers to know anything about my life, because honestly, it wasn't a life. If I wasn't at work, I was in bed. I didn't think there was anything in joining Facebook for me. I was wrong.

I joined Facebook in January of 2012. This is the first post I made: "It's a new year and I have a new theme song. I've been 'sitting on the side lines' since I lost my parents and now there's no reason to wait for tomorrow. I just love this song!" and I linked the post to Mandisa's "Waiting for Tomorrow" which partly goes:

> I can't live my whole life wasting/All the grace that I know You've given/'Cause You made me for so much more than/Sittin' on the side lines/I don't wanna look back and wonder/If good enough could've been better/Every day's a day that's borrowed/So, why am I waiting for tomorrow

In other words, I was ready to get in the arena and shake it on the dance floor! After joining Facebook, I found safety in closed groups where I could share what was on my heart without fear of my boss or my family members seeing the posts. Initially, I was drawn to depression and other mental health groups, because that's where my vibration was. I met some amazing people in the groups and even saved a few lives using nothing but my words and the power of my story. At the same time, people I met on the internet saved my life (and sometimes my ass) over and over again. In short fashion, I was hooked on Facebook. That's when I switched from watching crime dramas in bed to collecting memes and virtual friends.

In 2013, a year in advance of my son leaving for college, I joined a closed group for Empty Nest Moms. A day or two after being inducted into the sacred and secret group, it was clear I was different than 90% of the other moms. Go figure! Many of the other moms were heartbroken, sad, and feeling a lost sense of purpose after their children left for college. Me? I couldn't wait for my son to leave. The prior years, which included my seven-year stint in bed, were really challenging for me and I wanted a break. While I was a little afraid of the potential reaction from the other moms, I made a bold post in the group expressing my true feelings. Thankfully, Laurie, another Empty Nest Mom, reached out to let me know I wasn't alone. We chatted endlessly through messenger and on the phone, learning we were both single moms of only sons. We were also both adult orphans having lost both of our parents. Chatting with Laurie added new dimension to life. It wasn't long before we declared one another "sisters from another mister" and formed the Smart Wild Kinky Mamas group so we could go out and dance.

Dancing has a similar social component as the internet; it's actually even more natural and easier to navigate—especially at clubs like Denny Arthur's. I remember talking to a group of men who were experiencing Denny's for the first time. They were surprised by how friendly the people were and how chill the environment was. I mentioned to the men that I could just start dancing with complete strangers and I would be accepted into their group. They didn't believe me. Of course, I took it upon myself to show them. I bounced right onto the dance floor and began shaking it with a group of middle-aged women I'd never seen before. Of course, they welcomed me with hugs and smiles. The men were shocked! On another night, my friend Silver Becky took the challenge up a notch when she grabbed my hand and pulled me into the middle of another group's dance circle. Not on the side, mind you; she pulled me right into the middle! I was a bit terrified and had no idea what to expect, but we got down in the middle of the circle nonetheless. Instead of shaming us and kicking us out, the circle was surprised, but elated. Everyone had a good laugh.

That's exactly what collaboration feels like—even when it's done with strangers you meet on the internet or on the dance floor. I invite you to dance. I invite you to collaborate with friends and strangers alike. This world is so small and online connections turn strangers into friends and dance partners. Fear says we won't be accepted, it won't go well, or it couldn't possibly be that easy, but I disagree.

We are powerful creators and connectors who can help others live in ways that are joyful, abundant, and free. When wondering if your story has the power to change lives, it's easy to think "I can't do it alone." Collaboration gives you purpose, power, and influence. Together, as Smart Wild Kinky Mamas, we changed our own worlds and surprised many people by doing "outrageous" things like connecting with strangers and dancing in circles with an attitude of, "Why the fuck not?"

TranscenDANCE	
Jump into the middle of someone else's dance circle and get down.	
TranscenDANCE statement:	Get into the arena and on life's dance floor.
TranscenDANCE prompt:	Make a new connection online by reaching out to someone you respect or can learn from. Be genuine in your outreach and let them know why you're connecting. Challenge prompt: Go dancing join in the line dances or jump into the middle of someone else's dance circle and get down.
TranscenDANCE Spotify playlist:	**Line Dances** bit.ly/LineDancesPlaylist Line dances are one of the best ways to socialize with strangers on the dance floor. Practice with this playlist.

Hard times require
furious dancing.
— Alice Walker
TranscenDANCE

Chapter 9

Brilliant Transformations and Dance Circles

The Universe led me to start my own business after losing my corporate job. The rebel in me decided to call my business, Brilliant Transformations. Here's why: About a month before losing my corporate job, I impressed myself with an out-of-the-box solution to a problem we'd been plagued with for months. I exclaimed to my CEO boss, "I'm brilliant!" His dry reply was, "You're not brilliant. You're good. But you're **not** brilliant." I was crushed and a bit dumbfounded. I mean, even if he believed what he said to be true, which for the record, is not, it certainly didn't need to be said in such a blunt manner. At the same time, my mind and body were transforming before my eyes. Having lost 110 pounds from a strange digestive disease, I could cross my legs for the first time in years. I began wearing dresses and completely replaced my wardrobe with fashionable and sexy attire. Even my med doctor took note, greeting me saying, "Hello butterfly, I think it's time we back off your meds."

Thanks to the friends I met online and the Smart Wild Kinky Mamas group we formed, I had a crew to dance with every weekend. Many of the women became, and still are, great friends of mine. We traversed many outings including movie nights, day trips, and meals out; but the essence of our gatherings centered around dancing at clubs.

In recovery, I earnestly turned to dance to "flap my wings." It was the stress relief I craved and the grounding I desperately needed. Most times, I honestly didn't care to meet, to seduce or be seduced by anyone—although that occasionally happened. I genuinely enjoyed dancing with my girlfriends or by myself. Something about recovery, my new figure, and most importantly, my **need** to dance gave me the courage to do what I never considered before. Suddenly, I was confident enough to rush the dance floor at Denny Arthur's and shake my ass, even when I was the only person on the floor. I wasn't the least bit concerned about what other people thought. I was determined to take care of me and that meant dancing every chance I could.

Dancing alone is freeing. At the same time, it can be an act of rebellion. It's unexpected and bold. Sometimes I think I send the world a big middle finger when I dance alone. It's a "Fuck you, I'm not waiting for you, I'm not depending on you, I'll take care of my own needs, and I'll make my own damn fun." In many ways, my habit of dancing alone was born out of the trauma and drama of not fitting in, and refusing to conform to social mores. I was driven to dance more than any expectation I could encounter or refute; I simply followed my heart and did what I needed for me.

I considered that progress. And yet, there were casualties. Not everyone understood my need to flap my wings. When I initially recovered from depression and dropped weight faster than I could accommodate, people, like my twin trauma, only saw a new "me" emerging. They didn't see the sickness, the sleepless nights, the endless worry, the excessive tears, and the way I struggled to renegotiate the way I showed up in the world. It took several months before I was able to stop myself from crying when people would comment on my drastic weight loss. The fact was, while I needed to lose the weight, I didn't choose to lose the weight. I was incredibly sick. Plus, after being invisible to men because of my obesity, my shrinking body invited attention I hadn't experienced in years. I suppose that's why the sexual interest I received was challenging. Even within my own circle, cursory judgment and jealousy grew and became difficult to manage. Things came to a head one night when a friend of mine left the bar in tears because a guy *she* talked to asked for *my* phone number. Another friend dug a knife in my heart with her frustrated plea, "We want our fat friend back!" It wasn't long after this incident before our larger circle dissolved.

I've heard it said, "Women are bitches." That's sometimes true. But, have you ever met strangers in the women's restroom of a dance club? They're the nicest souls you'd ever meet. In restrooms across the US, I've seen female strangers offer kind words, lipstick, tampons, condoms, breath mints, a shoulder to cry on, and cold, hard cash. Some are even saintly, holding another woman's hair while she vomits. Friends, I've found, are the ones who fight; strangers, not so much.

When the cattiness appeared within my dance group, I recall declaring, "There's enough for everyone. There's no shortage of men, women, love, and relationships." It was as if the group suddenly believed there was a limited amount of goodness in the Universe and no one was entitled to have more than anyone else. As a gaggle of dancing women, it also became hard for some in the group to reflect genuine happiness for another's wins. Sadness, though, was covered in droves; commiseration became the norm. While commiseration is compassionate, it wasn't the encouragement I was looking for. Happiness seemed more challenging to support and encourage. I suppose it was because that's what was more natural for us. Like me, many people are trained to be comfortable with discomfort. Free Spin: Of our larger group of 10, the woman with the tears and the one who made the insensitive comment are the two friends I still talk with the most. These women are not bitches. They are human. Trust, honesty, and forgiveness are beautiful things.

I remarked earlier that I used to hate movies where everything is lovingly wrapped up by the end. You know the movies I'm talking about. I was frustrated by movies like *Pretty Woman*, *When Harry Met Sally*, and *Notting Hill* where the girl gets the guy and they live happy ever after. I didn't hate the movies because I hated the idea of them. In fact, I desperately wanted to **be** happy and in love like the couples on the screen. However, I didn't see myself ever experiencing that kind of relationship, so I became angry and envious seeing other people in loving relationships. The possibility of a loving, satisfying relationship simply didn't register for me. In Law of Attraction terms, a loving relationship didn't resonate with me because I wasn't a vibrational match to one. There wasn't anything wrong with me, I just wasn't there yet. To be clear, my dream life always looks like I'm thin, happy, wealthy, and enjoying a loving relationship. Even today, it's clear I'm not the perfect vibrational match for a smoking hot body or that quintessential love because I have not attracted and maintained them. That is, not yet.

This past summer, I read *Pussy, A Reclamation* by Regena Thomashauer, who is known in life coaching circles as Mama Gena. In "The Pleasure Revolution" chapter, Mama Gena talked about inner radiance and Sister Goddess Activism. Essentially, this is a process where turned-on women hold one another accountable to their higher potential. The problem with women connecting in this way is that, in America, we've often learned to see radiant women as a threat. Remember the whole "women are bitches" thing. This thought pattern has been engrained in our psyches. To avoid being labeled a bitch, and to avoid threatening their friends by talking about their great jobs and amazing relationships, otherwise strong, bold women will often lead instead with bad news, drama, and negativity as a connection point. Everyone can relate to drama and negativity; and women are no exception. Plus, when a woman connects with friends experiencing a lower vibration from the same frequency, there's no fear of a friend "stealing" problems in the same way they could steal a date, a dance partner, a job, or a man. Mama Gena notes, "This kind of cultural agreement [between women] is another form of enslavement. It binds us to negativity, instead of our potential." I totally agree and, clearly, the women in our Smart Wild Kinky Mamas group attempted to perpetuate that enslavement, albeit unknowingly or unconsciously.

Instead of troubling the dance floor with negativity, TranscenDANCE brings new potential to life—and new potential is a helluva lot more fun with genuine, compassionate, supportive people by your side. I absolutely love the way Mama Gena describes community:

> We need each other. But it is not the neediness of old; it is not the neediness of dependence and desperation. It is not the neediness of mutual victimization. I need you to be as big, blazing, and radiant as you can possibly be. Because the more of your legendary light you step into, the more of mine I can inhabit and embody. By standing in my own sacred radiance, I open up room for you to stand in yours—beyond the parameters of what you or I can imagine.

It can be uncomfortable to step into the light. My absolute favorite representation of friends stepping into the light is as a dance circle. Sometimes you're in the middle of the circle strutting your stuff while a league of people surrounds you and cheers you on. Most times, you're part of the circle creating a net of support for the person in the middle while they shine.

Have you noticed the dance progression of people entering the center of a circle? While the first few people are extra courageous in getting the party started, they are also often pretty low-key with their dance style. They may move their hips and their shoulders a bit, but it's nothing too fancy. As soon as one dancer really gets down in the middle of the dance circle—maybe they do the worm or breakdance a bit—the people who dance in the circle after are just a bit more "out there" than those who went before. That's courage. And it's catching while the intensity and fun of the dance rises with each new person in the center. That's radiance. That's light. It's my belief we need more courage, radiance, and light in our lives. Dancing is a way to achieve that.

TranscenDANCE	
Support others to be their best selves.	
TranscenDANCE statement:	TranscenDANCE means we celebrate, lift up, and support others.
TranscenDANCE prompt:	Watch the 2020 Super Bowl Halftime Show with Jennifer Lopez and Shakira! Write down any judgments, critiques, and comparisons that come up for you. How can you reframe criticism to bring value, support, and love?
TranscenDANCE Spotify playlist:	**Girl Power Reflections** bit.ly/GrlPowerPlaylist This is an extensive playlist with really great tunes. It's not exactly "chill," but also not exactly dance music. It's a great reflection of radiance.

Your body is the ground
metaphor of your life, the
expression of your existence...
So many of us are not in our bodies, really
at home and vibrantly present there. Nor
are we in touch with the basic rhythms
that constitute our bodily life. We live
outside ourselves - in our heads, our
memories, our longings - absentee
landlords of our own estate. My way back
into life was ecstatic dance. I re-entered
my body by learning to move my self, to
dance my own dance from the inside out,
not the outside in.
—Gabrielle Roth

TranscenDANCE

Chapter 10

The Slow Burn of Ecstatic Dance

On a beautiful Sunday afternoon, I attended an ecstatic dance event in Los Angeles. Ecstatic dance was the first outing I indulged in after moving across the country from Iowa to California. One of the best things about Los Angeles is the extreme deluge of events. I can pull up Facebook on any given day and find 1,000 things to do near me to fill nearly any desired need. Seriously, anything you want to do here—no matter how strange—you can find an event and a like-minded tribe.

A couple weeks after moving, I'd gone as long as I possibly could without dancing; my tank was on empty and I was adamant about finding a dance floor. There was just one problem; it was Sunday. Free Spin: In my hometown of Des Moines, it would be difficult to find any sort of dancing on Sunday. The town took a cue from *Footloose*, maybe. Whatever the reason, Biblical or civic, there was little to no dancing outside of Friday and Saturday nights in Des Moines. In Los Angeles, the internet took all of .005 seconds to find me an invitation to an ecstatic dance event later that same afternoon.

> I was intrigued by the ecstatic dance invitation. It read:
> *What is the dance that is seeking to express itself through you? Celebrate with movement, music, health, joy and community. Bring your love to the dance floor as this will for sure be an illuminated occasion!*

"Illuminated" severely understates ecstatic dance; "ignited" might be more apt. When I arrived, a spark led to a blazing fire in me and I was thrilled by how powerfully dance was reintroduced into my new life in the biggest city on the West Coast.

I showed up early and could feel how overdue I was to dance—by at least two full weeks. I chatted with two men in the atrium as soon as I entered and each pulled out a handful of crystals from his pocket then proceeded to discuss crystalline properties with me. Crystals are thought to have healing powers and help promote certain feeling-states. I subscribed to this notion years ago. However, in Des Moines, I never once ran into a man who carried crystals. Let alone one who felt comfortable sharing such New Age beliefs with others. Here I was among a diverse tribe of long-haired men talking about something I loved. I was intrigued and comfortable as fuck when the thought hit me, "These are my people!" Mainly because, when I talked crystals in Des Moines—especially with men—I was met with extremes: either glazed eyes or witch-labeling. Neither felt good.

I did, however, feel a bit left out because I didn't have crystals to share. Although, I *was* wearing a rose quartz yoni egg. Unfortunately, I couldn't pass that around in the same way as the men were sharing! It was good for a laugh, though. Free Spin: Yoni eggs are egg-shaped crystals inserted vaginally for greater pelvic tone and orgasmic response. You'll read later how they help me with dance.

When it came time to begin to dance ecstatically, we were ushered into the studio barefoot. Multiple Yoga mats were laid out in a circle; many of the regulars brought their own. We enjoyed a half hour of very gentle yoga movement, which I'm not very good at because I'm not terribly flexible. But I didn't get frustrated like I normally would and some of the easing movements were similar to QiGong, which I'm familiar with, so I did okay with the warm-up.

Like an anxious lover who pays no attention to foreplay and goes straight to penetration, I was ready to get my groove on. Never mind the yoga pre-game, I was getting blue balls! But, fuck: eternally slow-moving dance was next. Not-so-ecstatic. The 20 or so dancers there were floating around the room, back-and-forth, almost as if underwater, ballet-style, each in their own little world. The energy of the room was pleasantly light but much different to the sexually-charged Iowa clubs I was used to. Each person danced independently and unconcerned with their surroundings. In clubs, I was used to "peacocking"—seeing and being seen—where folks put themselves on display. At ecstatic dance, only a handful of the dancers moved with others. There was no pressure, primping, or preening. I began to wonder if the spark would ever flash more fully; for now, it was almost laughably contained.

But soon—the tempo of the music sped up, maybe incrementally, but suddenly it was there. And the dancers' energy followed suit. Rhythm, movement, and originality upticked. And I mean original. People totally had their own vibes going; one woman did somersaults, one after the other, like a tireless acrobat; one man did a handstand against the wall and pumped up and down like a jackhammer—like his arms were his legs. A couple decided 1950s swing moves were apt; hula hoops orbited hips; someone skipped to the music across the floor. Others jumped up, beaming, arms raised in Hallelujah like they were getting church. The spark was now a crackling bonfire. And all the while, I took it in, feeling more than thinking, "This is the epitome of LA."

I moved to the coast for exactly this reason. Dr. Phil might call this a "target-rich environment." For me, it was about being with people who like to do the same things I like. I was having fun; I was building the potential to meet others, socialize, and build my support base 1,700 miles west of where I'd spent most of my life.

As slowly as the night's process began, it ended super-quickly. It was as if a hose had doused the ecstatic fire. I was literally saddened; probably a little shocked it was over. One minute, dudes are running around in circles, seemingly high as kites, the next, I was about to make my exit. And for the record, no one was high. The event was completely drug- and alcohol-free, promoting only mindful living, veganism, and energetic healing. Hence, the crystals.

Sad as I was, it had been truly ecstatic; I couldn't stop smiling per usual when dancing. But, wait! To my surprise, the whole slow spiritual immolation began again. The dancers were once again fanning the flames ever so slowly. Patience has never been my strong suit. But my sadness was dispelled and the experience caused me to coin a meme: "Life is a constant reminder we will never get 'There'—Patience is required."

Ecstatic dancing actually taught me to slow down! To savor time. So often we are in such a hurry to get wherever we are going, we forget about the joys that take place along the way. That night amongst the ecstatic dancers reminded me that we never really arrive at *the* destination. It's the dance instead that we can learn to enjoy along the way, however slowly the movement may sometimes progress.

TranscenDANCE	
Place yourself in a target-rich environment for your future self—even if that means moving across the country.	
TranscenDANCE statement:	It's easier to find people and situations we connect with on a soul level when immersed in a function or culture or tribe that resonates with who we are.
TranscenDANCE prompt:	Find a target-rich environment and explore! Check out Meet-Ups.com and Facebook events to find people who like the same things. Set a date to go to an event—or two, or three.
TranscenDANCE Spotify playlist:	**California Vibes** bit.ly/CaliforniaVibesPlaylist Get in the spirit of California—Issa Vibe!!

It's the heart afraid of breaking
that never learns to dance.
—Xiaolu Guo
TranscenDANCE

Chapter 11

Protected

One of the group instructors I encountered recently noted, “Leads propose moves, they don’t impose moves.” It’s the same way with the Universe. We are given gentle, subtle guidance constantly. But often we are so tied up in our own heads that we miss the cues. If we ignore these delicate proposals for too long, it may get to the point where the Universe will “impose” a brand-new reality—just like it did with my divorce, my chronic illnesses, and the loss of my corporate job. Initially, these impositions feel and look negative. I mean, who would cheer for some of life’s toughest transitions like divorce, chronic illness, and job loss? However, these sequences were essential parts of the dance that led me to a better life.

While I failed to miss the initial lead and change my reality before the Universe stepped in with changes that gave my life new direction, I’m grateful for the redirection because I’m now enjoying a more aligned and joyous dance through life. The wake-up calls I experienced were harsh but obviously necessary.

After experiencing several of LA's best clubs and epic dance and music events, ecstatic dance still called me. During the time I visited and now returned, the ecstatic dance community grew exponentially and the practice became more popular. Two years later, the quaint Westwood studio I'd participated in was filled with not dozens of dancers, but hundreds. The practice was also expanded with interpersonal connection exercises. Not surprisingly, the day I returned, a partnered dance experience offered a lead, and a lesson, from the Universe.

For the experience, dancers were paired and given a blindfold. One of us was to wear the blindfold and express themselves through dance, while the other was to keep the blindfolded dancer safe among the crowd of other enthusiasts. My partner, until then a stranger to me, was resistant to the activity and didn't want to fully participate. She stated in no uncertain terms that she wouldn't be wearing the blindfold.

I don't know why she came out to ecstatic dancing and was reluctant, but whatever. I volunteered to be blindfolded first to at least get us some momentum. My dancing started slowly as I inched around, moving my body as if contained. My partner placed her hands on my shoulders and directed me to unobstructed spaces on the dance floor. I soon became more confident in my expressiveness, taking up more and more space and moving with more purpose, despite having no eyes.

The more I moved, the less my partner directed my steps. This confused me. At one point, likely a trauma response, I straight up thought she ditched me because I couldn't feel her hands, I couldn't hear her voice, and I couldn't read her presence. My movement was uninhibited; yet I simultaneously felt betrayed and abandoned. Because she wasn't constantly validating my experience through sensory input, my insecurity caused me to wonder if my partner rejected the exercise and me.

In the midst of my free-form, ecstatic expression, when I felt most alone, I received a slight nudge on my shoulder. It wasn't directional like the ones my partner started with. This was more of a tap with a suggestion to veer in a different direction. The touch was gentle, almost sensual, and affirming. Her touch reminded me that she was still with me. In fact, she was there the whole time. I couldn't see her. I couldn't feel her, but she was by my side. Her hands-free direction provided me the space I needed to dance freely and passionately. If only I trusted my expression and felt grounded by her ever-present support, I would've enjoyed the experience so much more.

Because I was looking for input from my partner—whose guidance I likened to the Universe's—her gentle touch was enough to move me in a new direction. Dancing and expressing helped me be in my body enough to feel the subtlety of her touch and make corrections to align my movement and flow. Being so delicately guided into and through the process ensured I didn't need a more forceful reminder to stay safe in my expression.

A good life, like a good dance experience, is one where we've tempered our doubt with faith. When insecurity and doubt arise as they inevitably will, they can be mitigated with faith, certainty, belief in ourselves, our calling, and the unique expression we were born to deliver. Life's dance involves moving courageously and enthusiastically while trusting in the support and guidance provided by our lead, the Universe. Support is buoyed with the knowledge that even when you feel alone, you aren't alone. Dancing with the Universe means knowing that there's always another possible move after a misstep. Accomplished dancers know some of the best choreography is derived from errant turns. And dance duos know help will always be provided by their partners. They're open to receive assistance and they understand that help may look or feel very different than what they expected. People who trust in the lead of the Universe know assistance arrives perfectly on time—not a moment too soon or too late. They consistently follow the lead and take the steps, even when they're unsure or unfamiliar with the routine, knowing they will be supported in their life's Dance.

TranscenDANCE	
Be uninhibited and accept directional nudges as they arrive.	
TranscenDANCE statement:	Allow yourself to be led by the nudges of the Universe and trust in its protection.
TranscenDANCE prompt:	Blindfold yourself and dance, ideally with a partner who can gently give direction and keep you safe.
TranscenDANCE Spotify playlist:	**Breathe** http://bit.ly/BreatheRelaxPlaylist This is the playlist that will calm a racing mind and remind you that you are protected. I often listen to this when I go to sleep.

If you dance with
your heart,
your body will follow.
—Mia Michaels

TranscenDANCE

Chapter 12

Individual Stance

It wasn't until I was over 30-years-old that I learned the value of being "planted" like an oak tree in my truth. During my most hellish job, things came to a head in a big way. In October of 2004, I had major surgery to correct a work-related injury. After asking multiple times for a headset, my employer failed to provide one—while requiring me to be on all-day-long conference calls when only a portion of the call applied to me. Our work was fast-paced, and I was tasked with more work than I could possibly manage on my own. Being the master multi-tasker I am, I spent days with my ear constantly positioned on my shoulder to hold the phone while I did computer work. Working repeatedly in this position exacerbated an existing neck injury from a prior car accident. It wasn't long before my right arm was constantly numb. The fix wasn't an easy one. I had a cervical fusion where my bulging C5/C6 disc was removed and the vertebra were fused together with cadaver bone and a metal plate. The work was secured with four screws in the front of my neck. The recovery was as challenging as the surgery. It was a full 12 weeks before I was released to return to work. During this break, my depression took an interesting turn while I was at home. That is, it flipped; I became manic, staying up all hours of the night to do ridiculous things like laundry, clean the carpets, and clean the oven. The funny thing is, because I was usually depressed and in bed, our house in Iowa was generally messy. Why I became obsessed with these obscure cleaning tasks was beyond me, and yet, I couldn't stop. When I told my psychiatrist—I called him my "head med doctor"—that I had taken the oven doors apart to clean between them, the bipolar II diagnosis came out. This is when the combination of medications I was on took a sharp turn and anti-psychotics were added into the mix to better help me chase woke and beg sleep.

I returned to work in January. Two short months later, on St. Patrick's Day, way-too-drunk me fell face-first while hailing a cab for home at the very late hour of 7 pm, only a few hours after my mom dropped us off at the bar. The fall broke my wrist and required another surgery. The orthopedic surgeon recommended six weeks off work to recover. I still felt guilty leaving my coworkers for 12 weeks for my neck surgery during our busiest time of year. Plus, I was really ashamed that I needed surgery because I sidewalk dove while intoxicated. As a result, I scheduled the surgery for a Friday morning, so as not to inconvenience my boss or coworkers or take any time off. Can you say codependent? I returned to work angry, disheartened, and resentful of others when I was the one who created the situation by getting face-plant drunk and then compounded the situation by failing to take care of myself because I was so ashamed. Meanwhile, I continued to do my best at work; I kept meeting everyone's needs while ignoring my own.

I had no idea what to do with the discomfort I was feeling and I was even more challenged by how to properly express it.

From the time I was a toddler, I was constantly told I was "too sensitive" or "always dramatic" whenever I expressed emotion. Nearly all emotions, especially negative ones like anger and disappointment, were not welcome in my home. So, I learned to suppress most of them. As a result of being told to hide or ignore my feelings my entire childhood, I regularly chose to prioritize other people's needs instead of my own as an adult. Given the option of betraying myself for others or standing in my own truth, I always chose the former.

Thankfully, during this time I had a spiritual advisor teach me about "righteous anger," which was a totally new concept for me. She explained righteous anger as anger that serves a positive purpose—usually to initiate a change of some kind. Protests are forms of righteous anger and she encouraged me to stand up for myself, that is, stand tall in my truth. Who knew? I certainly didn't. Standing up for myself meant having difficult conversations with the leadership team about my workload while taking personal responsibility for my choices, like drinking too much, and making newer, better decisions. Less than a year later, I took a near 50% pay cut to leave that job in favor of better work-life balance. That turned out to be one of the best decisions I ever made. While I took a step backward in pay, the forward trajectory of my life was positively altered, and put me on a completely different path.

That same concept came full circle at dance class, recently. It was only a few weeks into my private lessons with Stephen when I felt the advantages of appreciating my individual stance in dance. While practicing turns, Stephen did a turn on his own. He let go of my hands and turned away from me. He'd never done that before. When coming back to me after his turn, he exclaimed, "Congratulations! You kept doing your own thing and allowed me to do my own thing. When I did something different, you didn't lose a beat with your steps."

Oh, wow.

That was **big**—and a very important reminder. Even though he did something new and different, we remained connected in the dance. As we continued dancing, it was important for me to have independent, yet consistent movement. I surprised myself by not getting tripped up when Stephen did his own thing during our dance. I can't tell you how many times I get tripped up—off the dance floor—when things go differently than I expected. The most obvious example in life is in my romantic relationships. But, I am also similarly confounded by friendships and work relationships. Instead of standing in my power, my truth, and my independent movement, I turn inward, internalize problems, overthink, or make "corrections" to meet another's needs—not realizing their actual need is for me to be **me** and continue doing my thing.

In sharp contrast to how I learned to move freely on the dance floor, when I'm off it, if I'm not centered or present, I tend to hibernate in my mind. I overthink most everything. My son calls this doing the "Mama 500." He says it's like I'm lapping a racetrack, running the same loop over and over. On the Mama 500, I spin out faster and faster with no reprieve, so my son's description is spot on. When I'm on the Mama 500, I'm oblivious to the greater opportunities life has in store and I tend to ignore my own gifts.

Thanks to the freedom dance provides, I know for sure what's it like to live off the Mama 500 racetrack. The way I experience myself, the way my awareness grows, my life looks and feels very different when I'm grounded and focused. I find this place of peace when I'm open to an exquisite balance between being literally rooted like an oak tree and flowing with the stream like a piece of driftwood. It's being poised to shift when aligned and standing firm in my own personal truth. Mostly, like an oak tree, this stance feels joyful, grounded, and certain—no matter what. This certainty is coupled with an infallible belief in my own abilities and a matching conviction in the Universe's ability to literally move me with ease and grace.

TranscenDANCE	
Stay rooted in your truth.	
TranscenDANCE statement:	Being rooted entails connecting to our body and bringing awareness to our mind. According to Ilchi Lee, in the book *Connect*, by performing soft, repetitive movements like tapping, a calm vibration is created and the mind drops (along with the endless chatter of thoughts) into the body.
TranscenDANCE prompt:	In a sitting position or lying on your back, with legs touching, lightly tap your feet together. Focus on inhaling then exhaling to expel energy, tapping about 100 times, moving the energy down into your toes, giving your mind a break. Watch the "Body & Brain" YouTube video on toe tapping for additional direction. bit.ly/BodyBrainTapping

TranscenDANCE Spotify playlist:	**Rooted** bit.ly/RootedPlaylist These songs are meant to connect you with the earth and your truth.

Meeting in the middle allows two bodies and souls to join together and create one dance.
—Stephen Thomas

TranscenDANCE

Chapter 13

Meeting in the Middle

Dance is energetic. It creates energy, allows energy in, disperses energy out, and effectively responds to like energy from other dancers. The best dance partners act as mirrors for one another. Two individuals move as one, interrelated equals with opposite but collaborative expressions. With dancing, the emotion is palpable, the flow is vital, and the sensuality is electric.

My instructor Stephen said this about the language of dance: "Dancing with a connection is about having a conversation. I believe partner-dancing is a language in itself, and the actions and reactions are words, sentences, and conversations." In my experience, this conversation takes place while navigating the continuum of 100% cumulative effort. Individual partners create a space where they bring everything they have to the table. They show up at 100% while allowing their movements to meet, match, mirror, or reverse the action of the other. On occasion, one partner may move 80% forward while the other moves 20% backward. However, the overall dance is balanced and the shared equity goes back and forth instead of one person consistently "efforting" while the other remains still. Can you imagine a dance where one partner is standing still and the other is dancing all around their partner putting in all the work? That's not a dance, that's a laughable display that lacks reciprocity, and fails to include fluid reactions from one partner to the other.

Speaking of equal and opposite reactions, let's go back to codependency for a moment. I was married from 1993 to 1998. My son was two when his father and I separated after a lover's getaway gone bad. We went to Kansas City in an attempt to recapture the magic and broke up on the way home. The day after my husband left, we had our first marital counseling session. It was an appointment I had made weeks before—our first as a couple. I went alone. My husband was done with me and our marriage and refused to go to the appointment. I remember saying, "If you'd just tell me what's wrong, I'll fix it. But you leaving without giving me a chance to work things out isn't fair." Of course, my immediate reaction was to assume responsibility and take ownership of making necessary adjustments to get the relationship "on track" when it never was even on the rails in the first place. It's funny to me the way I was willing to "fix myself" in order to revive a relationship I had no desire for in the first place. Even though I didn't want to be married—and had told my husband as much months before he left—I still felt obligated and loyal to marriage because that's the example my parents set. You stay married. Period. Even when you're unhappy—especially if you have kids.

Showing up to counseling alone was hard, but necessary. I wanted to make some sense of the impending divorce and single parenting, and I wanted to get some sure footing to continue on and make a good life for my son. My depression was evident and medicated, but somewhat manageable at this point. From my perspective, I was functional. A few weeks before the split, my mom said to me, "I'm so glad you're not a single mom. You'd never make it." Now, here I was, a single mom with a mom who didn't believe in me. I have no idea what prompted her to say that and it certainly pierced my soul, knowing the breakup was coming. Although the deck was seemingly stacked against me on that Monday morning, I showed up to our counselling appointment anyway. Consistently showing up alone in life—to parties, work events, school sports, parent-teacher conferences—would prove in time to be even more challenging. However, this resilience, persistence, and stubbornness to show up in faith when things are falling apart around me has proven to be one of my greatest strengths.

I'll never forget the counselor's description of how partners should interact with one another. Using his hands, he described the totality of 100% effort in partnership. On the far left is one partner. The other partner is on the far right. Good relationships work when both partners consistently meet in the middle. He placed his palms together in the center of his chest to represent 50/50 effort. He went on to show what was happening in my marriage. I was the right hand rushing to the far left while efforting all over the place. I planned dates, encouraged sexy rendezvous, and tried to talk about our situation—incessantly. I cared for my partner's needs on the left while ditching my own position and passion on the right. The counselor moved his hands from right to left and left to right showing that less effort on one side invites the other side to do more and balance things out. The counselor went on to say, "When everything is 'done' for you [meaning my husband], there's no need or desire for you [again, husband] to do for yourself." It's like when you're a kid and your mom cleans your room, does your laundry, and cooks for you. As kids grow, non-codependent moms stop doing all the work and give their children the opportunity to do things for themselves, in the way that serves them best. At this point, the counselor suggested less effort on my part may lead to more effort on my husband's part to balance things out.

In the case of my marriage, it was too late to tell if less effort on my part would've led to a better-balanced relationship. However, I know for certain this balancing act is true—thanks to other experiences in my life—especially when it comes to letting the Universe lead. If we have everything figured out, how can the Universe step in to surprise us? I've found this to be true in dating. When I try to manage everything with care and attention, I fall into the masculine role of leading. This automatically creates an imbalance and either chases men away, or puts them in a position where they feel like they can't do enough or do anything right. This scenario is frustrating and exhausting for both of us. However, when I step back and lessen my efforts, and step into the feminine role of being led and allowing a man to care for me in his own way, those who are truly interested step forward. Those who don't, weren't all that interested in the first place, and it's a good opportunity to let them go.

One of my favorite examples of this is from the first man I dated after my divorce. We were going on a picnic and grilling steaks. I'm kind of particular about steak and I wasn't sure he'd marinate it. Instead of trying to take charge, I stepped back and let him handle all the barbecue details. Not only did he marinate the steaks, but his scratch-made marinade was far better than a store-bought one I would've used. He also brought a Caesar salad and dessert. I was totally surprised and delighted, all while doing less, allowing the date to unfold, and letting my date lead.

The concept of getting more while doing less is foreign to the way I was raised. And yet, that's what happens when we are open to receiving, and letting the Universe lead.

During one of our early sessions, Stephen and I talked about the stance where dance begins. Just like a relationship, it's about meeting in the middle. When we dance, my left hand is on his shoulder and our right hands are palm to palm, to my right and forward. This dance stance is not at all dissimilar to the emotional stance the counselor demonstrated in that session right after my husband left. The totality; 100% built on equal participation. Because partner dancing was new to me, I didn't feel strong in my stance and often retracted in response to the energy my partner advanced. When the instructor met me in the middle, I instinctively fell back into myself. It was hard for me to maintain my offering. Again, this was mostly habitual codependency in action. I was used to both overcompensating for the perceived "failings" of my partner and experiencing discomfort when someone is both competent and willing to meet me in the middle. Especially in those early dance lessons, I was neither used to being me in all my glory, nor allowing a partner to show up in all his glory. My desire for a healthier dynamic with an aligned and invested partner is exactly why I signed up for the therapy of dance education and practice.

And boy did I need it! Instead of waiting for and following the lead, I found myself anticipating what was next and "covering" in the same way I did in my marriage. Stephen gave me further insight into being proactive in dancing, which helped me feel better about my intention to help. He noted, "Reading what the other person wants and needs is an asset in dancing—as long as you get it right by not rushing or going early, but waiting until they are ready—so you can join them in doing it together." I've always been great at anticipating needs and jumping in to help. Except, I nearly always did it from a place of 100% efforting while not allowing others to give their contribution. What Stephen taught me is that, in the same way we listen before rushing in with commentary when someone is speaking to us, in proactive dancing we join our partner in their expression as the need, movement, and direction are clearly conveyed.

Of course, that happens with the Universe, too. Sometimes we get a glimpse of our power, begin to doubt ourselves, and fail to maintain our stance. A few short months after moving to California, I quit the only steady, paying job I had. It was a small $1,500 stipend and it was work that I loved, but I was no longer aligned with the organization I worked for. Abraham Hicks talks about these situations as contrast, noting, "When you know what you don't want, you know what you do want." The experience presented so much of what I didn't want that the contrast was evident. I put in my notice without a thought. Instead of focusing on the loss, I started to write what I did want. That writing became a draft of a personal, spiritual manifesto about a collaborative culture I wanted to create. When I wrote it, I knew it would be a TED Talk. The ideas were fresh, inclusive, and downright inspiring. After I wrote the first draft, I let it sit and breathe. I didn't stress about it. In fact, I didn't put any effort toward it, I knew it would come to fruition in the right time. In other words, I trusted the Universe to lead.

A little over a year after I completed the manifesto, on March 30, 2019, I delivered my TEDx Talk, "The Dance of Collaboration," at Pasadena City College. It was one of the best experiences of my life. I wasn't the least bit nervous. I felt like I was born to give that talk. My son attended and seeing him beaming in the audience was the best feeling ever.

On my 48th birthday, 45 days later, my talk was released to the public. I expected to be the next Brené Brown, immediately. Like with most expectations, that's not how the events unfurled.

Before my talk was released, a good friend asked me, "What if nothing changes afterwards?" I honestly hadn't considered that. I was planning to be like Brené, jet-setting around the world sharing "The Dance of Collaboration." Sure enough, when that didn't happen, I retracted. I isolated and fell into a deep depression. I forgot to surrender to the Universe's lead. There's nothing wrong with feeling disappointed, but I only prepared for one outcome. When that outcome didn't occur, my depression grew bigger than the lifetime of depression I experienced before. This left me feeling completely ashamed and uninspired. Why? Because I knew better. And so, I started beating myself up. I know plans take time to develop; I know things are always working out for me—especially when they don't appear to be working out for me. And yet, I resisted everything. I turned inward, doubted myself, and nearly abandoned everything. For the first time since the depths of my despair after losing my parents, the suicidal ideations resurfaced—with a vengeance. My psyche's reaction was unrelenting for months on end. It was both shocking and embarrassing. From the outside looking in, my life was great. I just crushed a powerful TEDx Talk, moved into a new, luxury apartment in Fullerton, southeast of LA, and was attending as many fun events as I could. Meanwhile, I was spinning and found it hard to get through the day. Even though my ego was talking mad shit and imposter syndrome haunted me, I continued going out, getting social, and dancing as much as I could. I also made a point to connect with virtual and Facebook friends in person. These outings were just the reprieve I needed to keep going.

Because of the seven years I spent in bed while depressed, I knew this time around to only get in my bed to sleep. I spent most of my time lying on my bedroom floor in a lovely "nest" I created with my heated amethyst BioMat. I napped frequently, listened to meditations, and compulsively watched YouTube videos about codependency, healing, ascension, and trauma. I worked only on client business and did nothing to advance my dream of becoming the next Brené Brown. Despite my failure to realize my dreams, I managed to stay alive, keep breathing, complete client deliverables, and experience periods of deep rest.

During this process I learned that to provide adequate support, the Universe needed me to show up and maintain my stance as an active participant in my life's dance! The Universe can't move me forward when I'm not paying attention to its subtle leads and intuitive nudges. Just like the woman who guided me while blindfolded, the Universe was helping me, despite my belief that I was alone. Before I could fully move forward, it was necessary to pause, listen, and pivot. When the movement and direction of my life's dance was clear to me, the hidden language of my soul was unleashed and the narrative of this very book, *TranscenDANCE*, came to life.

To get back to dance, I was called to surrender—accept what is—and give up the idea that things should unfold any differently than they were at that moment in time. It meant letting the Universe lead. Gabby Bernstein, the author of *The Universe Has Your Back,* sums this up perfectly in her latest book, *Super Attractor*, stating:

> The Universe is always conspiring to support you, guide you, and compassionately lead you toward the highest good. When you're focused on chaos and fear, or trying to control everything, you deflect this support and guidance. But the moment you surrender, the Universe is there to pick you up off the floor and show you the way.

More importantly, getting off my bedroom floor and transitioning back to the dance floor required repositioning myself toward joy. It was time to meet the Universe in the middle and let the Universe know I was ready to be led.

<table>
<tr><td colspan="2"><h1>TranscenDANCE</h1></td></tr>
<tr><td colspan="2">Do the work to meet your partner in the middle while your partner does the same.</td></tr>
<tr><td>TranscenDANCE statement:</td><td>Showing up to do the work, maintaining our stance and being active participants in life’s dance requires trusting that we are not alone. Staring into the mirror, we see that we are whole, complete, and loved by the Universe.</td></tr>
<tr><td>TranscenDANCE prompt:</td><td>Mirror work: Write down several affirmations to say out loud. Some examples include, “I am enough,” “I am loved,” “I am open and receptive,” “I am following my dreams,” “I choose to dance,” “I accept the lead of the Universe,” “I surrender,” and “I trust my intuition.” Choose a time when you will be undisturbed and sit/stand in front of a mirror. Gaze in the mirror at your reflection for a minimum of five minutes. Repeat your affirmations with feeling. Embrace the emotions and thoughts that come up for you. Repeat this daily for 90 days.</td></tr>
</table>

TranscenDANCE Spotify playlist:	**Shine** bit.ly/ShinePlaylist We can only meet a partner as deeply as we've met ourselves. This playlist will help you cultivate and radiate self-love.

Consciousness expresses itself through creation. This world we live in is the dance of the creator. Dancers come and go in the twinkling of an eye but the dance lives on.
—Michael Jackson

TranscenDANCE

Chapter 14

Present and Available

During my TEDx Talk, I exclaimed, "We are powerful creators and connectors who can help others live in ways that are joyful, abundant, and free." I strongly believe we are here to express ourselves, share our gifts, and lead the way for others to do the same.

Author Robert Scheinfeld agrees with me. In his book, *Busting Loose from the Money Game*, he describes the human ability to create absolutely anything we want. He states, "As an infinitely powerful, wise, and abundant being, you have an unlimited desire to express creatively and fully experience the expansion and joy that comes from that expression. In fact, as you'll soon see, all of human life is essentially about creative expression, no matter what it looks like." In case you weren't sure, my favorite form of creative expression is dancing because it releases stress and brings me joy.

Do you know what Gabby Bernstein, the author of *Super Attractor,* says about joy? "When you lean toward joy, you are led!" That's what happens when you show up to dance. Sometimes you're led by a partner. Many other times though, you're led by the spirit within. **Movement and expression offer freedom—when you're present and available.**

I once dated a man who was very spiritually-advanced. He was tuned into the Universe and had an open and expressive pineal gland. Also known as the third-eye, the pineal gland is an endocrine gland in the center of the brain. When awakened, the pineal gland is associated with intuitive wisdom. This man was very perceptive and also recognized and believed in my magic. While we didn't connect on many levels, he had amazing intuitive abilities, which I admired. Not long into our relationship, we had a date planned at the end of the day. As a codependent and needy partner, I was pushing for more couple time. When I asked about the time between the end of his work day and the start of our date, he surprised me by asking, "Do you want me to show up at your house full of the worries of the day, or would you prefer that I be empty, free, and clear so we can enjoy one another?"

I honestly couldn't imagine the idea of my mind or body being empty, free, and clear. Most especially, my mind is rarely quiet. According to Deepak Chopra, it's no wonder my mind races considering the number of thoughts we have every day. However, Chopra asserts meditation as an answer to this, noting, "Meditation is not a way of making your mind quiet. It's a way of entering into the quiet that's already there–buried under the 50,000 thoughts the average person thinks every day." This is what my date was trying to do in the space between work and seeing me.

While my date's commitment and suggestion to be clear was new for me, I understood it—in theory. I most certainly didn't understand it in practice; because the Mama 500 runs through my head near constantly. As I've already mentioned, I have a hard time being in my body. I'm used to numbing it, stuffing it, or excessively worrying about it.

When we show up for dates, whether they be on the dance floor or elsewhere, it's important to have a clear body and a quiet mind. It's the same way with the Universe. It's hard for the Universe to move us when our bodies and minds are cluttered with junk—hence the literal clearing and excreting that happened in my life when I got chronically ill and lost 110 pounds.

My buddy Eric Cedeno, a surfer, takes this a bit further connecting the purpose of dance to other modalities observing, "Dance, martial arts and surfing have a lot in common. The ultimate goal for all of them is the same—to be in a state of flow. Where you can react to anything at the subconscious level and free your mind of all other thought so that you can live in the present."

One of my private lessons with Stephen made this real for me and reminded me to be "empty, free, and clear." It happened when he manipulated my arms for additional styling and poise. He stood near me, with me, and essentially remade me into a puppet who moved to his rhythm. My arms were at his mercy as he created beautiful poses and arrangements. I liken this to the way we can show up to be moved by the Universe. When we are free, clear, and pliable, God can move us in ways that provide the highest good for everyone involved. In essence, we become the dance the Creator brings to life. The gift we deliver to others by accepting our life on the Universe's lead is our legacy.

Michael Jackson changed the world of music and dance and his legacy will live forever. Had he cleared his personal clutter and exorcised his pain, while creating such a movement, his legacy might have been more fondly remembered by the masses. However, in light of the allegations against him, his life's work—however grand—became forever tainted.

I love what former comedian and actor turned best-selling author and transformational speaker Kyle Cease says about the way we are rewarded through alignment and doing our inner work. In his book, *The Illusion of Money*, he talked about the way the Universe led him to his career change noting, "This planet is evolving into a higher vibration of love, generosity, compassion, contribution—the more you get in sync with that vibration, the more life will see you as a collaborator in its evolution and give you the resources you need to make as big of an impact as you are willing to make."

In order to make the impact I plan to make, I continue to show up with love, generosity, and compassion and to share my contribution. Often that means being flexible enough to drop my resistance and allow the Universe to move through me.

TranscenDANCE	
Follow your joy to a state of flow.	
TranscenDANCE statement:	Being in a state of flow is being led by joy and immersing ourselves deeply in something we are passionate about. We feel free, lose track of time, and open up energetic pathways when we are in the flow. One example of this is singing!
TranscenDANCE prompt:	Sing! In the shower, in the car, at karaoke, wherever it feels good!
TranscenDANCE Spotify playlist:	**Anthems** bit.ly/TDAnthemsPlaylist Anthems are songs with lyrics to live by. You'll feel confident singing them.

Every dance you make belongs to you. It is part of your collection. When you think of it like that, you'll want to make your next routine the best you've ever made!
—Torron-Lee Dewar

TranscenDANCE

Chapter 15

Choreography and Movement

If you didn't know this about me, I'll tell you now: I'm a perfectionist who likes to control things. I also strive to be the best at nearly everything I do. In fact, I remember a therapist telling me once, "Melissa, don't just take therapy as something else to be perfect at."

His caution was very indicative of my character. And so is the following story, one of the most telling of my life. When I was about five years old, I wanted to take our dog for a walk. I couldn't find the leash and my mom was too busy to help me. I was angry. I hadn't been taught to write yet, but I scrawled a note to my mom that said, "I hate you." She read it and spanked me. It was the only spanking I ever received, because I was a near-perfect child, (as far as she knew). Afterward, I sat under the dining room table and cried. Then suddenly, I blubbered, "B-but...did I s-spell it riiiight?"

Meaning, the exasperated note I'd left her. There I was, double-checking if I expressed myself correctly, despite being in the wrong and, per my mother, deserving of corporal punishment. I was expecting perfection as a pre-kindergartner without even yet having proper training and experience with writing. How perfectionistic of me. For the record, I did spell it right; writing and editing have always been two of my natural gifts.

Here's the problem and the point of my youthful anecdote: When we're over-controlling, when we're in a perfectionistic stance, we're not open to be led by the Universe's dance. It's the same thing as one individual contributing 100% of the collective effort: it doesn't give others a chance to do their part. I used to consider taking responsibility for a person or a group as leadership. When it comes from a place of alignment, I believe that's true. However, I've found that often my "leadership" comes from a codependent place. In that case, it's enabling, which is the opposite of leadership.

One of the best things about dance—especially socio-spiritual environments like ecstatic dance—is the ability to try new moves freely without feeling self-conscious or inclined to perfectionism.

As I kid, I wanted so badly to take dance lessons. I took gymnastics for a short time, but never dance. I always felt like the children who grew up in dance had advantages I didn't. First, because dance studios covered a lot of neighborhoods and demographics, my friends there had an additional, separate crew of dance class friends outside of school. Second, they were learning how to be more comfortable and adept at moving their bodies, which became especially helpful back at school when trying out for cheerleading, drill team, and dance troupes. Especially compared to the dance kids, I struggled with realizing fluid movement and capturing dance routines. When I attempted to dance back then, it was generally excruciating, emotionally and physically. Everything felt very contrived and looked very unnatural. In junior high and high school, I tried out for everything but I only made it as a flag girl, which, in high school, was the antithesis of the glamor the dancers and cheerleaders enjoyed.

Many years after my reticent flag girl days, I finally took a dance class that was new to me: hip-hop—my first ever. In one short hour, the dancehall instructor, Tango Leadaz, taught our small class a specific routine to the song "Toast" by Koffee. The song is reggae with a quick beat and Jamaican slang. The lyrics and melody exude gratitude and the first part of the dance is called "Congrats." It's a literal happy dance.

> Yeah, we give thanks like we need it the most/We haffi give thanks like we really supposed to, be thankful!/Blessings all pon mi life and/Me thank God for di journey, di earnings a jus fi di plus/Yeah, gratitude is a must, yeah

While I love to move, I'm not quick to learn choreography. There was a woman in front of me who picked up on the routine immediately—it came to her as quickly as the instructor introduced it. She embodied the routine instantly! Me? I kept asking him to repeat the instruction and give us more time to practice. I was embarrassed and a little ashamed I wasn't catching on quicker. And my steps were not even close to perfect. That didn't stop me. I completed the class and consoled myself by noting that the woman and other participants likely took many more dance classes than me. I did really well for a first-timer. Plus, I had a blast, was grateful to be invited by a friend, and was proud of myself for sticking it out and not quitting when I got frustrated.

Another consequence of missing dance classes as a youngster was missing the camaraderie that comes with rehearsals. The idea of performing on stage for an audience was thrilling to me, as I'm sure it is for so many dancers and entertainers. The costumes, the make-up, the updos and fancy hair, the flowers, the stage lights, and the applause were all so appealing. Even the gruelling practices that lead to the performance seemed like fun to me. Because so many of my friends and later, their children, took dance, I've attended years of performances. The larger, well-known studios had rehearsals at the Civic Center—Iowa's largest theatre in downtown Des Moines. My friends and their doting families dedicated entire seasons and weekends to dance performances. I was a proud supporter who also carried a significant amount of envy toward the dance experiences my friends enjoyed with the families.

Like the quote in the beginning of the chapter asserts, every dance is part of our collection. We learn bits and pieces from different places and different people. Sometimes it's a "slow, slow, quick, quick" start at lessons and other times it's a full-blown routine. When we let the Universe lead, we accept each dance, each performance, and each love for the richness it adds to our lives, regardless of our expectations or of unexpected outcomes. Gabriel Marcia Marquez reminds us that, "No matter what, no one can take away the dances you already had." Knowing the memories of dance, love, and performances reside in my heart give me comfort and make me excited about the new routines I can co-create with the Universe.

TranscenDANCE	
Take new dance classes, feel foolish when you're challenged by the choreography, and refuse to quit.	
TranscenDANCE statement:	In order to experience the Universe's dance, we must relinquish control and perfectionism. Learning a new dance while feeling self-conscious and refusing to quit offers new found freedom and courage.
TranscenDANCE prompt:	Watch a YouTube video of "Fitness Marshall" and dance it out! Don't worry if you can't keep up with the choreography. Have fun! For an advanced prompt, go to a dance class like line dancing or hip hop and challenge yourself to stick with it.
TranscenDANCE Spotify playlist:	**Work It!** bit.ly/WorkItPlaylist This playlist curated by my friend Vanessa is all about being motivated to dance it out (or work out).

When the music changes,
so does the dance.
—African proverb
TranscenDANCE

Chapter 16

Life's Soundtrack

The more I come alive through the lead of the Universe, the more important role music plays in my life. Often, I wonder if music is what brought me to life. Then, more often, I turn that question into an acknowledgment. Music *is* an integral part of my recovery from more than 20 years of depression. Of course, music and dance are inextricably linked. The beauty of music, especially music with awesome lyrics, is that it transports my mind and heart to new places—regardless of whether or not my body moves.

Music's muscles hang on the skeletons of lyrics and it's the lyrics—the poetry behind the song—that often move me, internally, spiritually; and of course, externally, via dance. In fact, the more intimate I am with my recovery, and the more I trust my intuition, the more I'm able to tune into an entirely new musical frequency. This new frequency is one where the Universe literally sings to me. I can be working, writing, or contemplating something, when I'll hear a snippet of lyrics that syncs perfectly with what's going through my head and heart. I often use lyrics in the articles and social media posts I write because they are inherent in my message and provided with Divine Timing.

Not long after quitting my stable job in California, I met Evan Stein, a music artist manager, through a business connection. Over a seriously long lunch, we talked extensively about music. I loved the way he talked about music and the way it "soundtracks" life. He's absolutely right. It's nearly impossible to hear a song and not be instantly transported to the time and place most closely related to that song. Older songs can take me back to the roller rink, junior high dances, and high school parties. Not only do the memories of the song come rushing back, but the feelings do, too. A song like "Heaven" by Bryan Adams will transport me to Skate West where I'm surrounded by prepubescence, Pac-Man and Asteroid video games, Tombstone pizza from the toaster oven at the snack bar, and giggly girls hoping to be chosen for the romantic partner moonlight skate.

The instant feelings instigated by a song aren't always welcome. Sometimes songs transport me to a different place that's not always happy. In this case, a song will put me back into a vulnerable position, if it's associated with a previous love, a dark time endured, or the loss of a loved one. I celebrate the progress of healed wounds when I hear songs that used to send me to a sad place without also returning to the pain once associated with that tune. I celebrate even more progress when I feel gratitude for the pain experienced in a sad memory. Music invites me to revisit even darker, more difficult memories with fresh eyes and an open heart.

The very first song on my life's soundtrack is one I visit often. It's also a song associated with pain, but I believe our greatest pain brings us our greatest insight. “Free” by Prince, from his early masterpiece, *1999*, has incredible insight for the challenging times many of us endure. Prince sings:

> Don’t sleep ‘til the sunrise/Listen 2 the falling rain/Don’t worry ‘bout tomorrow, don’t worry ‘bout your pain/Don’t cry unless u’re happy, don’t smile unless u’re blue/Never let that lonely monster take control of u/Be glad that u r free, free 2 change your mind, free 2 go most anywhere, anytime/Be glad that u r free, there’s many a man who’s not/Be glad 4 what u had baby, glad 4 what u’ve got

I remember, in high school, lying on the floor of my basement bedroom, cranking this record and letting the tears flow after my first boyfriend broke up with me. I cried with the song many times after that. Even today, when a romance doesn’t work out as planned, “Free” is my go-to song to remind me to be grateful that I’m in charge of my own destiny and thankful for the lessons and experiences I gain from each encounter.

Maybe 10 years into my major depressive episode, “It’s Been Awhile” by Staind was ever-present on the radio and steady on my playlist. Its lyrics haunted me: “It’s been a while since I could say that I wasn’t addicted/It’s been a while since I could say I loved myself as well as you.” While the song appeared to be about a lost love; for me, it was about how long it had been since I’d taken care of myself. It was a not-so-gentle reminder to start paying more attention to myself, hence, “It’s been a while since I could hold my head up high.” By that point, I’d been a single mom for four years. I was working full-time and going to school full-time to finish my degree in business management. Even though my employer paid 100% of my tuition costs, I incurred $20,000 in student loan debt. As a single mom, I had no problem qualifying for loans. And as a single mom, I had no problem spending the disbursement. Sadly though, I spent much of the money frivolously. At the time, I was going out every Wednesday night after class, and every other weekend—when my son was at his dad's—binge-drinking, and making questionable choices. I refer to dancing during this period as "back in the day." It was fun for sure, but it came mostly from an unconscious place and was not the healing salve it later became. "It's Been Awhile" was a nagging reminder that I needed to do better. I wanted to "hold my head up high," per the lyrics, instead of repeatedly doing the walk of shame.

A few years later, "Unwell" by Matchbox Twenty became my theme song. I had embraced my crazy by this point. There was no doubt I was in the throes of major depression and was even diagnosed as bipolar II for a period. Life was spiraling out of control and I had no idea how to maintain it. The funny thing is, if I had released control, accepted myself, and surrendered to the lead of the Universe, I would've spun less. I hadn't come to the point where I understood that control is an illusion, and I certainly wasn't ready to relinquish it. Depression for me was a matter of everything and nothing at the same time. It's like nothing is really wrong, but at the same time, nothing is right, either. From the outside, my life looked good, but inside I was revolting. My body was growing larger, topping out at 307 pounds and my mind was crowded with obsessive thoughts. Matchbox Twenty's lyrics summed up my life at the time perfectly:

> Hold on, feeling like I'm headed for a breakdown
> and I don't know why/But I'm not crazy, I'm just a

> little unwell; I know right now you can't tell/But stay a while and maybe then you'll see a different side of me/I'm not crazy, I'm just a little impaired; I know, right now you don't care/But soon enough you're gonna think of me and how I used to be—me

From there, the shit hit the fan, so to speak.

I lost both of my parents in the same year. In a turn of events that are only visible to me now, I was introduced to greatness at their respective funerals. In 2017, two members from my church, Lutheran Church of Hope, competed on The Voice. We were blessed to have both of these superstars sing at my parents' funerals; John Mero sang at my mom's funeral and Chris Weaver sang at my dad's. They each sang "Amazing Grace" in the soulful, heartfelt way only they can.

While losing my parents is the greatest loss I've endured to date, further seeds of belief and grace were planted in this experience of their passing. Particularly after my son left for college, when I was no longer caring for my parents and my son, I had no choice but to take care of me. That's when I started connecting with others and dancing.

I started listening to contemporary Christian music in 1997. It was after my husband left and I was honestly looking for a country music station because I wanted lyrics that had a message. The irony of the typical messaging in country music is not lost on me. Here I was looking for hope from a genre of music that's known for broken relationships, broken trucks, and broken people. By the time I lost both my parents in 2011, I listened exclusively to

Christian music because it comforted me with lyrics focused on promise, faith, and redemption for anything and everything "broken."

In late 2014, as I've mentioned already, I contracted two violent, concurrent chronic illnesses, and I did my best to maintain my director-level position reporting to the CEO of an insurance company while being incredibly sick. "Just Be Held," a song by Casting Crowns gave me the hope I needed to keep doing my best and its lyrics went:

> Hold it all together, everybody needs you strong/But life hits you out of nowhere and barely leaves you holding on/And when you're tired of fighting and chained by your control, there's freedom in surrender, lay it down and let it go/
> So when you're on your knees and answers seem so far away, you're not alone, stop holding on and just be held/Your world's not falling apart, it's falling into place/I'm on the throne, stop holding on and just be held

I didn't know it at the time, but this song is a perfect representation of allowing the Universe to lead. I remember working exhaustively until 11 pm at the office one night and listening to "Just Be Held" on repeat for hours. It sustained me. A month later, my corporate position was eliminated—and I was relieved! I recognized my dismissal as a blessing not even in disguise. Though it looked like my world was falling apart, it was finally falling into place, with the Universe leading the way.

As I had done almost unknowingly many times before, I surrendered and opened myself to new and different beginnings. A month later, I heard "My Story" by Big Daddy Weave for the first time and bawled immediately. It goes:

> If I told you my story, you would hear hope that wouldn't let go/If I told you my story, you would hear love that never gave up/If I told you my story, you would hear victory over the enemy/If I told you my story, you would hear freedom that was won for me/If I told you my story, you would hear life overcome the grave

Listening to that song, in that moment, my purpose became clear to me—I overcame the "grave" of depression, suicide attempts, and suicidal ideation to live a life of freedom and help others do the same.

In the fall of 2014, Walk the Moon demanded us all to "Shut Up and Dance." Dancing became a way of life for me—a healing revelation. It increased my vitality; became a necessary form of stress relief; was a means of introducing me to amazing friends; and it gave me something to look forward to each week. This song was released around the same time I was coming into my own and transition from a severely depressed state, spending seven years in bed, to dancing every weekend. I often tell people to "shut up and dance with me," literally as we're teetering at the edge of a dance floor or in the broader sense anywhere else, wherever there's a place or circumstance I want to take them to, a trust or bond I'm hoping to instill. There was no looking back—my life was on an entirely new trajectory and I decided to dance my way through it.

When I started dancing in 2014, I also started listening to secular music and my playlists went from exclusively Christian to a much wider range that included an occasional gangsta rap song. After all, my Millennial son and I share a lot of music. My playlists are much like my life; diverse, emotional, and a bit all over the place. It's fitting that my current life soundtrack is populated with rap. "California Love" by 2Pac is the sonic elixir representing all the goodness and badness that moved me here to the Golden State. The pain in my life literally packed my boxes and drove me out West. I believe every single thing we experience, including the pain, is a nudge toward our purpose and our best life—if we can perceive it that way. Following love, loss, depression, and song, I decided my best life was in California. On Independence Day, 2017, I moved over 1,700 miles from Des Moines, Iowa to the Los Angeles basin. Free Spin: On the drive out, I shuffled **all** the music, blaring it so much I blew out the speakers in my new car.

TranscenDANCE	
Open yourself up to new tunes and genres of music as you evolve.	
TranscenDANCE statement:	In order to experience the Universe's dance, we must tune into the frequency we want. Like a radio station, our life's music can change and evolve over time.
TranscenDANCE prompt:	Create a soundtrack for your life. Write about the top 10 songs that frame your life.
TranscenDANCE Spotify playlist:	**My Soundtrack** bit.ly/MySoundtrackPlaylist This is a playlist that's as diverse as my recovery journey. It includes all the songs mentioned in this chapter.

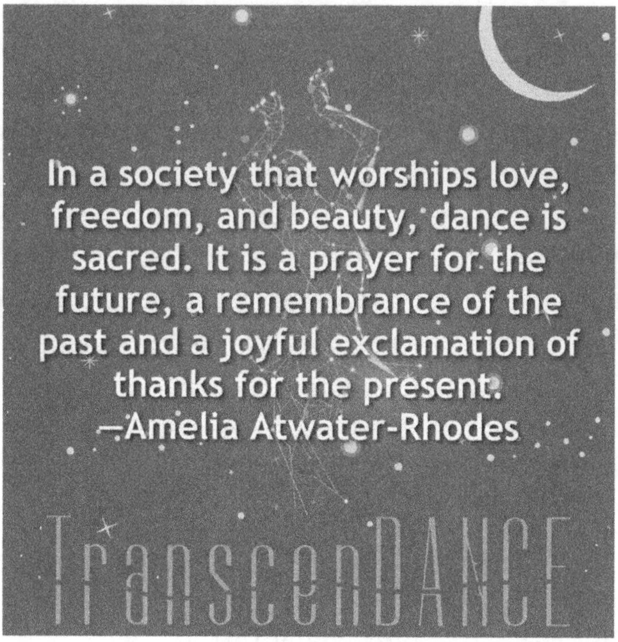

In a society that worships love, freedom, and beauty, dance is sacred. It is a prayer for the future, a remembrance of the past and a joyful exclamation of thanks for the present.
—Amelia Atwater-Rhodes

TranscenDANCE

Chapter 17

Patient Anticipation

In 2012, my son and I took our first vacation after losing my parents. We flew to LA and stayed with family. We spent a week touring beaches, seeing the sites, and exploring the city. My son was 17 at the time. He was so excited about the city and exclaimed he would move to California one day. I replied, "I would never live here." I mean, I was all set up at home. I owned a home and had a great job. Here's the real story: once I got home from work, I wasn't leaving my bed and living in California was "work." I was so exhausted during our trip, I took a nap every day. I seriously couldn't imagine living at such a vigorous pace day in and day out. Life in Iowa was safe and comfortable. I knew what to expect—until I didn't. Free Spin: My son moved to California a year after I did. As much as I love the city, he now despises it. He's in love with California, but now prefers the slower pace and lessened traffic of the Inland Empire (about 40 minutes northeast of where I live).

My corporate job loss in 2015—three years after our Cali trip—was something I didn't expect. At the same time, I welcomed the change. I knew I needed to leave my job. I liked my work, and I was exceptionally good at it, but it didn't feed my soul. I remember an energy healer saying to me, "You've invested 100% of your heart into your job. Are you sure insurance is where you want to place your heart?" My exact response was, "Fuck no." But, I had a very large bonus coming, an all-expense paid reward trip to Costa Rica scheduled, and a hysterectomy looming. Shit was happening in every corner. My plan was to ride out the job for a few months and then start looking for something new. When I was presented with a severance package, I took it as a lead from the Universe. While I didn't have the slightest idea what I would do to replace my income, I wasn't the least bit worried about it. Honestly. I trusted my job loss as a blessing, promptly got a new tattoo that said, "Everything Happens for a Reason," and proceeded to jump into the abyss of the unknown. Free Spin: My son and I both got "Everything Happens for a Reason" tattoos. Mine is written in his handwriting.

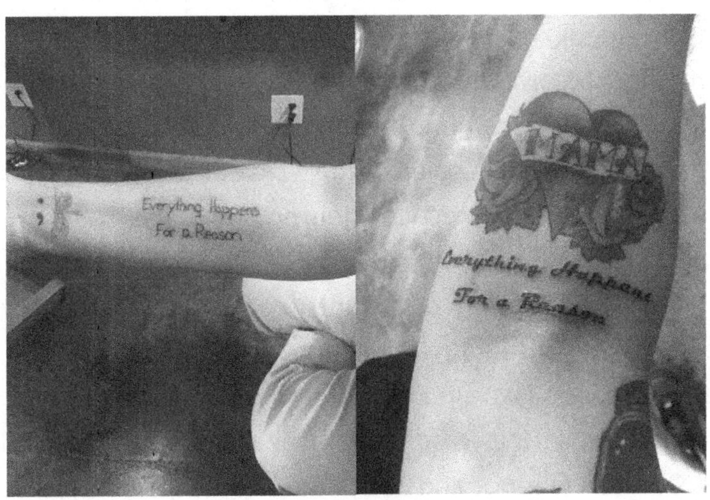

Around the same time my position was eliminated, my body and mind were experiencing what I termed a "brilliant transformation." Having lost 110 pounds from the digestive disease, my physical body was metamorphosing in a way I hadn't seen in decades. Digestive-supporting probiotics also helped transform my mind and alleviate the depression. (The gut-brain connection is real!) A few short months after leaving my job, I worked with my med doctor to begin the process of stopping all my mental health drugs.

The day after my last day at the office, I had a hysterectomy that resolved my second chronic illness. Interestingly, getting let go from the insurance company spontaneously resolved my first chronic illness, the digestive disease. After my surgery, I was only sick with the digestive concerns twice—both were times when I had to deal with my former employer. That's no damn coincidence.

Leaving the company provided an energetic clearing that resolved the illness without further treatment. I took a couple of months to recover from surgery and then sought a coaching certification with a company in Los Angeles as an opening into a new career. Since joining Facebook, I'd felt great reward connecting with others and helping them resolve life's tough transitions. Because I've been through so many transitions personally, it felt like a natural thing to do. Plus, the lessons I learned in the 12-week certification program supported my personal recovery journey.

In 2016, I took a cross-country road trip by myself. During the epic, solo, month-long trek, I drove from Des Moines to Los Angeles and back. I was in a committed relationship with my twin trauma before I left. It was the first true relationship I'd had in 17 years. Our love was hot and cold, but always passionate, intense, and sexually-rewarding. I ended the relationship before leaving on the trip, mostly because I knew the life of my dreams was in California. When I set off to live my dreams, I wanted to be free of anything that could potentially hold me back from fulfilling them.

The trip was ridiculously liberating, rewarding, and educational. I learned so much about myself: the way I was previously-oriented toward life, and the way I desired to live on a going-forward basis. When I returned, I wrote this about the most important lesson I learned: *I used to hate to drive at night, and in the fog. I think the reason I got so nervous driving in those conditions was because I'd get ahead of myself. I'd look too far into the distance and the lights, cones, and mile markers would freak me out. In sharp contrast, I took this trip mile by mile.*

They say you don't have to see the whole staircase to take the first step. Driving 4,500 miles is the same way—one mile at a time. Day, night, rain, shine, fog, no matter. I just kept looking straight ahead and concentrating only on what was directly in front of me—not around the corner, or over the bridge, or in the next time zone. On that trip, I stayed present. I was in the moment right here, right now. When I just accepted the road as it came, it was easy to navigate. Instead of constantly trying to chase it, catch it, or anticipate the next stretch. That's not to say I wasn't mindful and aware of what was happening around me, because I was. But I learned in a visceral way that I can only control my section of the road. I released the desire to control things outside of my path—fully understanding that my path opened up as I continued staying present, moving forward, and remaining focused on the end result.

I didn't know it at the time, but this perspective was a pivotal shift that enabled me to let the Universe lead. At the conclusion of the trip, I created three new mantras for life:

1. Live Your Truth.
2. Let Intuition Lead.
3. Make Shit Happen.

I've always been good at making shit happen. When I set my mind to something, I've made some of the most seemingly impossible things happen. No one expected me, as a 28-year-old mother making $28,000 a year, to buy a house on my own in Iowa, but I did. No one expected me to dismiss the employment search assistance offered as part of my severance package in lieu of finding a career I was passionate about, but I did. And for sure, no one expected me to sell my house and move across the US to pursue my joy, but I fucking did. Once I'm committed, making shit happen is a given. But living my truth and letting intuition lead were new concepts to me at the time—ones that stretched every boundary of my being.

It wasn't until years later that I saw the fallacy of these three collective mantras. I completed an extensive study in the Law of Attraction, listened to Abraham Hicks YouTube talks daily, and saw Ester Hicks in person on three different occasions. Making shit happen goes against everything the Law of Attraction represents. Making shit happen is also heavily tied to my proactive stance, my need to control, and my desire to make everything perfect. All of that combined creates a fuck ton of resistance and an inability for the Universe to step in and dance with me.

Abraham Hicks talks frequently about our "internal guidance system." Since moving to California, living in three different towns since arriving, and frequently traveling, I have no choice but to allow my literal GPS to direct me—even for simple trips like going to the grocery store. The thing is, I always arrive where I'm headed. Sometimes I'm directed a different route and sometimes I miss a turn and am given new directions. Recalculating! No matter what, I always arrive. Not always on time thanks to LA traffic, but I arrive. Because I'm a California transplant, I trust that Siri (and its sexy British man's voice) knows my route better than me. I trust that Siri has more knowledge of the area than I do. Every time I get in the car, I'm literally handing over my navigation and trust to the process. I'm not controlling, creating shortcuts, or navigating self-created detours.

I've been following Mike Dooley of *The Universe Talks* platform for a couple of decades. I remember his particular brand of Law of Attraction teachings vividly. He teaches followers to set a vision for an end result and then be open to it. In dance terms: be poised, present, and available. It's not up to us to determine how things will unfold. That's up to the Universe. It's the same thing as me leaving navigation to Siri. In both cases, it's important to be open to the unfolding. Here's why: most often, when an answer or reason is revealed to us, it looks completely different than we expected. So, expecting to make shit happen is the opposite of being open; it's controlling and closed. It's a cousin to the aforementioned bane of perfectionism. For this reason, my new life mantra #3 is "Allow Shit to Unfold."

Every time I drive, I allow shit to unfold without thinking about it. It's natural. I trust. I surrender to the process. However, when it comes to love, work, and personal development though, I'm still on my tendency to constantly push to make "It" happen—whatever that fabled "It" is. Last summer, I wrote about expecting "It" to arrive and what that would look and feel like and shared it with my new friends at Xanadu's summer camp. Xanadu is a SoCal tribe centered on wellness, education, deep connectivity, and green living. I connected with this organization when I attended a silent disco dance cruise they offered. When I attended Xanadu's summer camp island retreat on Catalina Island in the fall of 2019, I performed. While on stage, I talked about allowing shit to unfold and read the piece I'd written about trusting the lead of the Universe and waiting with patient anticipation for everything we desire to arrive.

So many attendees talked to me after my performance. It seems the concepts in my talk hit home with the audience. It resonated so deeply with one woman, she approached me in tears. Another sent me an email months later recalling the way the concepts I presented changed her thinking and the way she orients her life. A special conversation happened when Eric Cedeno, a surfer attending Camp Xanadu for the third year, approached me. He was someone I met earlier at camp. During our conversation, he asked me about my hopes and dreams. I told him I wanted to write, speak, and encourage others by sharing the trials I've overcome and the lessons I'm learning. He asked me if a million dollars would help me meet my goals. My honest reply was something like, "If I don't get my head straight, no amount of money will help." It's funny that after delivering such an encouraging talk about surrender, I was so personally discouraged. I believe wholeheartedly in the talk I delivered, and yet, my life felt like a mess. While I was talking the talk, I wasn't consistently walking the walk. I've found that's how things often work. The words we share and the lessons we teach are often the same ones we most need to hear. I often wonder if that makes me a hypocrite. I've decided it makes me undeniably human. And honestly, that makes the perfectionist in me very uncomfortable.

Patient anticipation—faith in action—and knowing that the Universe is leading me to the highest possible manifestation of my desire is the drive that moves me forward through the Dance. No matter how challenging things get in my life, I'm certain I'm led. When I get still, present, and quiet, I can focus on the next right thing and allow the dance to unfold one beat at a time.

TranscenDANCE	
Live your truth and let intuition lead; allow shit to unfold.	
TranscenDANCE statement:	Brilliant transformations take time and unfold one step at a time. The Universe has our back and is working with Divine Timing. Allow your intuition to lead and trust your inner guidance system, all while keeping the vision of your highest self in mind.
TranscenDANCE prompt:	Spend five minutes envisioning your future self. For the next 20 minutes, describe your future self and write down your truest desires. Words have power. Be very specific in detailing your future life! Meditate on your future self for the next 90 days.
TranscenDANCE Spotify playlist:	**Roadtrips** bit.ly/RoadtripsPlaylist Here's a collection of tunes you'll want to belt out while driving down the highway. This playlist was inspired by my epic, solo road trip!

Dancing is surely
the most basic and
relevant of all forms
of expression. Nothing
else can so effectively
give outward form to
an inner experience.
—Lyall Watson

TranscenDANCE

CHAPTER 18

Turn, Turn, Turn

While debriefing me about my just-delivered talk on patient anticipation at Camp Xanadu, my new friend Eric upped the ante asking, "Would $20 million help?" But I had the same response as before, feeling that if my mental state wasn't improved, all the money in the world wouldn't matter. I know from personal experience that money—or lack thereof—only amplifies the current situation. During one of the most joyous times of my life, I literally didn't have any money, a job, or even my own car. That was just a few short years ago.

At that time, I did a quick video about how I was feeling and shared my thoughts regarding a meme with this text: "You have to be ready for money, which means you have to be happy without it." I think that's true in a lot of things. When you think about relationships, when you finally get to the point where you're absolutely satisfied and content being on your own, that's when the relationship shows up. When you release your attachment to the things you desire, that's when your desires will show up for you. Even when I'm experiencing a period of financial lack, I have an abundance of faith. I have an abundance of joy; I have an abundance of purpose; I have an abundance of self-love. I have an abundance of belief in me. I have an abundance of belief in other people. I have an abundance of self-respect that I've learned and earned navigating life's tough transitions like divorce, death of loved ones, chronic illness, job loss, and parenting. I have an abundance of personal truth, the ability to stand in and speak that truth, an abundance of honor, and an abundance of intuition. I'm finding the more I follow my intuition, the more I'm rewarded. And that's a beautiful thing. I have an abundance of direction and faith as I trust the lead of the Universe. And again, the more that I follow the lead, step by step, mile by mile, the more signs I'm given, and I'm really enjoying that fact, too! So, while I may be experiencing a financial lack at the moment, I have an abundance of many other things that are far greater to me than finances—and I'm perfectly fine with that.

The Universe **loves** to work with a heart like that. Being in joy and steadfast in my purpose, regardless of the external circumstances, the Universe brought me from a place of financial lack in Des Moines, Iowa to one of great abundance in California in a very short period of time. I simply had to trust in the process, follow my joy, and remain in purpose to be rewarded with greater opportunities.

Remember when I said healing isn't linear or a light switch? Well, my life is a demonstration of that. Sometimes it feels like we've made it, and then...well, shit! In sharp contrast to the purpose I felt when I did the video and shared the above sentiments—in 2017 before I left Iowa—I was in a completely different place in September of 2019 at Camp Xanadu when Eric asked me about a financial gift. At the time, money was flowing and I experienced my highest income year ever. I was crushing a bucket list goal of attending adult summer camp in California—**and** I was the furthest I'd been from aligning with my purpose than I'd been since I moved to California. I was making a great living promoting the work of other people, but I was suppressing my need and desire to advance my own work. Particularly after my TEDx Talk didn't get the traction I expected, I failed to show up for me and support my purpose. More importantly, I was letting fear drown out my intuition—whispers from the Universe—and it was showing on my body. I'd gained back 80 of the 110 pounds I lost through chronic illness. The weight was a constant and literal heavy reminder that my life was out of balance. On one hand, I was ashamed of the way I looked and desperately wanted to change it. On the other hand, I was stuck on the Mama 500 spinning my wheels. Meanwhile, the more I ignored the hand of the Universe and the lead it presented while employing unhealthy coping mechanisms, the further out of balance my life became.

When Eric asked about bestowing me with a generous financial boost, I knew my spirit wasn't quite ready for it. My outward form was reflecting a really uncomfortable inner experience. I knew I had to make peace with my situation and set some goals to make a change before my spirit could make proper use of a financial windfall. All my failures, false starts, and imperfections ran through my mind. I was really uncomfortable accepting a financial blessing. Truth be told, I'm pretty uncomfortable accepting most anything I didn't create myself. In the same way that I prefer leading to following in dance, I'm a fantastic giver—not a great receiver, yet.

As I was stumbling on my words, and deflecting the gift, Eric told me he believed in me, my gifts, and my purpose. Next, he handed me the cash. It was a $20 billion dollar bill—in Zimbabwe currency. Banknote World, a collectible currency company, describes the $20 billion dollar bill as follows:

> If you can't have a billion dollars in your pocket, who says you can't be made to feel like [a billionaire]? Grab a 20 Billion Dollar Banknote issued by Zimbabwe a few years ago and consider yourself a billionaire. Though you won't be one for real, there's absolutely no restriction on feeling like one. You'll be on top of the world!

In the year leading up to our meeting, Eric set out to make 100 billionaires. He used the Zimbabwe currency as a conversation starter to connect with and inspire dreamers like me. As evidenced by my reaction to his question about having millions and billions of dollars, I wasn't stuck on the value of the money. Instead, I was blown away by his insistence of **my** value, belief in my potential contribution to the world, and the support he provided. That was our second conversation at camp and it marked the beginning of a very beautiful friendship.

The following day at lunch, Eric and I were talking about my performance, the wait for "It" to arrive, dance turns, and patient expectation. I honestly don't remember much about the specific words we exchanged, but the emotion behind our conversation was profound. I do know he was encouraging me to be *me* and step into my authentic power. While we were talking, something hit me hard and the tears started flowing. It wasn't long before I was sobbing and experiencing a full-blown breakdown/breakthrough.

Here's Eric talking with me and my friend, Linda Gordon who traveled from Florida to attend Camp Xanadu. This was after the Floatpalooza beach time and before I broke down in tears. You can see, Linda and I were both captivated by the conversation. Thanks to Jason Power for the awesome photo capture.

Eric told me he took dance lessons with his mom when he was young. I love seeing moms and sons dancing. I love dancing with my son Johnathan who is 24. We've even taken a few lessons together. As our conversation wound down, I asked Eric to dance with me. As we laughed and danced, my tears turned to joy and I boasted the biggest smile—that's usually the way it happens with dance. A friend and fellow camper, Linda Love, happened to catch our dance and snapped a few priceless photos.

The sheer act of dancing was enough to turn my sadness into joy. And while we danced, Eric helped me see my challenging time and lack of alignment in a brand-new light. As with everything I do, I like to go big! I want things to be over-the-top and out of this world. I generally don't give myself credit until things are signed, sealed, and delivered—which means done, successful, and buttoned up. In other words, I don't easily allow things to unfold or celebrate small accomplishments. Here's what Eric made clear: In my performance at the camp talent show, I talked about waiting for "the turn." From a dance perspective, I love flashy turns. I'd be super excited for a turn-and-dip combo.

However, six months after delivering my TEDx talk, there were no flashy turns in sight. There were no corporate contracts, no publishing deals, and no upcoming speaking engagements. Never mind that I crushed two prior speaking engagements, collected testimonials, and made some critical decisions about my collaborative partners going forward. Eric told me I'd been turning the whole time—except the turns were slight, subtle, and far from "flashy."

Sometimes, we are too close to our work to see the progress. There's nothing wrong with patiently waiting for the grand turns and having ridiculously high standards. However, we get tripped up when we're expecting grand turns with a short-term mindset. Particularly with a large vision, things don't come together in an instant. It's important to recognize the incremental steps—or turns, and trust that things are coming together in ways we cannot see. In my humanness, I'd forgotten to acknowledge the turns while discounting my worth and recounting my imperfections. In other words, I clearly had not surrendered to the Dance.

TranscenDANCE	
Remember to recognize the progress and subtle turns that aren't wildly obvious.	
TranscenDANCE statement:	The Universe is always providing for us, yet we sometimes have to be patient to wait for our "turn." Important factors like being ready to receive abundance when it comes and accepting gifts are all a part of the journey. A great way to encourage this is by giving to make space for receiving.
TranscenDANCE prompt:	With beautiful intention and the understanding that what we give, we receive, dispense 10 $1.00 bills throughout your community. You may leave them in the pages of a book at the library, under a rock at the park, or drop one in a crowded store!
TranscenDANCE Spotify playlist:	**Prosperity** bit.ly/ProsperityPlaylist This playlist is all about cash money! It's great for manifesting, entrepreneurship, and envisioning your best life.

Dancing is
a perpendicular
expression
of a horizontal desire.
—George Bernard Shaw

TranscenDANCE

Chapter 19

Alignment, Intimacy, Connection, and Flow

It's been said that great dancers make great lovers. There are many other stereotypes I can debunk, but let's stick with dance. Dance is seductive, for sure. Or, at least it can be.

I saw him across the crowded dance floor at Denny Arthur's. This was toward the end of my "back in the day" dancing period in 2008 and 2009. He was dancing alone and damn, he had some good moves. I was truly captivated. We danced, we dated, we fucked. I know that sounds abrupt and unsightly, but that's how it felt. Which was shocking, considering the way he danced. He's a smooth dancer. He's the only man I dated that I could partner dance with. As a dance lead, I found him to be inclusive, easy to follow, and supportive. As a lover, he was completely the opposite. I knew him as a lover who was selfish, in his own world, and concerned with his own pleasure, lacking compassion and reciprocation.

Our relationship unfolded during that super dark period where I was depressed and basically bedridden. As a direct result, I wasn't doing particularly fun things in bed, either. I wasn't present. Mostly, I slept and self-medicated to numb the pain of depression and the sheer exhaustion that consumed me as a single mother. Comfort in the form of a warm body was welcome; but more often than not, the encounters left me feeling flat, irritated, and unfulfilled. The five psychiatric meds I took daily didn't help. In that time period, life was out of control in every way possible and sex didn't produce the pleasure, orgasm, or connection I desired and desperately needed.

Our intimate relationship fizzled out after only a few short months. After the break-up, and to this day, we are close friends. Because of our friendship, I often reflect on a quote I once heard that said, "If two past lovers can remain friends, either they never were in love or they still are." In 2015 and 2016 when I returned to Denny Arthur's in my recovered, conscious state, years after our relationship ended, that same man I dated and fucked seven or so years earlier was intrigued by me. He asserted that, in our past dating life, I would've had more fun sexually if I was more like my new self. My new self was vibrant, awake, energized, and fully-motivated. But that wasn't who I showed up as during our relationship. And yet, even as a person going through recovery, I couldn't acknowledge his truth without voicing my own. When I did fully acknowledge and express this truth, he was surprised and appreciative (more on that to come).

When critical illness catapulted my recovery from depression, one of the first things I did was make a declaration to take life by the balls. Pun intended. Through research, yoni massage, and coaching with a sexologist, sexuality became a core function of my recovery, health, and creativity. I searched high and low for new sexual techniques, sensual products, and coaches who could help me in my quest to reclaim my sexuality. Being in a safe, committed long-term relationship with my twin trauma for the first time in decades provided the perfect opportunity to explore the side of me that had been dormant or used inappropriately through casual hook-ups for years.

With healthy sexuality as a central theme in my life, I showed up differently. I presented as less angry, more loving, more inviting, and bubbling with ingenuity while solving nearly every challenge the Universe presented. In many ways, tapping into this sexual power helped me feel invincible. This new presentation of my **self** was exactly why my former lover expected I'd have more fun if we tried sex again in 2016.

While sexuality was a new focus for me in recovery, there were other big changes, too. Namely, I learned how to set and enforce boundaries aligned with my truth. With a new disposition on my side, it was easy for me to rebuff my former lover's advances while staying true to myself. In the case of my former lover, the truth was, I had no desire to revisit any of his sexual "wizardry." I believe in magic. I do! However, I let him know in no uncertain terms that we were not sexually compatible lovers when I said, "Your penis isn't magical if you don't use it for anything else but your own pleasure." Were we good dancer partners? Absofuckinglutely! But lovers, not so much. And that's okay.

On the other hand, my favorite lover, the twin trauma I rekindled in 2015, was a hilarious dancer who bumbled across the dance floor. He didn't exactly have rhythm and his movements weren't smooth. We didn't even pair up well for partner dancing, however enthusiastically we tried. We specifically chose to take partner lessons together and, hilariously, didn't step to the same tune in any way. Nevertheless, I totally dug how he committed; he got onto the dance floor and did his thing! I loved how much he enjoyed himself, even if sometimes it took a little liquid courage. He had fun and we enjoyed time dancing together. And we had a fantastic time in bed. The sexual pleasure we experienced was off the charts; our bedroom connection was what dreams are made of. Outside the bedroom and off the dance floor, however, consistency in our connection was harder to come by—especially with me pushing for specific outcomes, controlling the situation, and failing to allow him to lead.

Sometimes I can get so caught up in one connection—in this case, the sexual one—that I fail to recognize a total lack of connection in other areas. My dance instructor Stephen says, "The more connection points you have, the easier it is to lead." Literally in dance, there's an obvious connection in our hands, our bodies, and our eyes. There's also a heart connection (even when you're not in love), and a mental connection. There can also be a spiritual connection. The most essential of all these, though, is the energetic one. And when any one of these connections is missing, the lead, the follow, and the performance can suffer.

I do have an appreciation for my life's storied experiences when thinking in terms of dancing. I'm certain that having some bad dances is better than having none. As with the collection of dances I've experienced with strangers, lovers, and friends, each dance is deposited in my bank of memories and will help me build a full dance routine for my life's journey. Each dance is a learning experience that moves me across the Universe's dance floor. It's no *Soul Train* line dance, though; sometimes the movement is forward, sometimes backward, sometimes side-to-side. It's a beautiful dance if I let it, but it's far from precise or perfect.

As I write this at my kitchen table, "Dancing with a Stranger" by Sam Smith is playing in the background. For me, the concept of connection is to practice more discernment. Dancing with strangers is fun. Developing friendships is fun. Sleeping with and committing to people with whom I share few to no connection points isn't fun in the long run. It doesn't create the growth needed to support the destiny and other shit I want to unfold. While I'm holding out for the partner who dances with abundant connection, equitable availability, and infinite love; I'm preparing my heart, mind, and body to accept and follow his lead.

TranscenDANCE	
Refuse to settle for dance partners and life partners who don't have all the connection points you need.	
TranscenDANCE statement:	Exploring partnership, personal needs, and pleasure, is a dance with a learning curve. Coming to beautiful terms with loving ourselves and our bodies, both on a physical and emotional level, is key to TranscenDANCE. You are your greatest partner!
TranscenDANCE prompt:	In a manner that is comfortable to you— self-pleasure! Get it on with your fine ass self!
TranscenDANCE Spotify playlist:	**Get It On** bit.ly/GetItOnPlaylist This playlist is filled with sexy (and explicit) tunes.

The only way to
make sense out of change
is to plunge into it,
move with it,
and join the dance.
—Alan W. Watts

TranscenDANCE

Chapter 20

Navigating Dance Rhythms

Life is a dance; an individual journey with twists and turns that move as fast or slow as your heartbeat. There's a rhythm and soundtrack with an incredible range of tunes. One thing is for certain: dance evolves. Or at least, it should.

So often, our junior high dances were awkward. I imagine the chaperones get a kick out of watching boys on one side of the gym, girls on the other, nervous, feet shuffling back and forth, and lots of shoe-gazing. I don't want to spend my life waiting on the side of the Universe's dance floor like that. While Stillwell Junior High provided that keen partner who had practiced-up before taking me to the Valentine's Day dance, my actual eighth grade formal threatened to suck bad. My girlfriend and I had a double-date dinner and arrived at the formal ready to boogie. Our dates excused themselves to the restroom and my girl and I waited. And waited. After a while, I searched around for the boys and found their boutonnieres in the garbage can. They didn't go to the restroom; they ditched us. Upset as I was, I didn't cry. Instead, I pulled my girlfriend out onto the floor and danced the night away. We had the best time ever and I even got a few dances in with my biggest crush, a hunky, star football player. My mom was so concerned when I later told her our dates bailed. But when I told her how much fun we had, her fears evaporated, and she was glad for my girlfriend and me.

That story has repeated in slightly different forms throughout my life; it's part of the process. Dancing through heartbreak hasn't changed; in fact, dancing is an integral part of my recovery from all my life's trials. That's the beauty of dance. Shitty scenarios like punk eighth grade boys ditching and 40-something divorced man-boys happen. Chronic illness, losing loved ones, job loss, all happens. None of us is immune. I believe these ups and downs are part of the dance, with each step getting us closer to the destination we desire. We may as well dance throughout the journey.

Dance is a consistent companion for me. However, because dance is more fun with others and takes some organizing and planning, there are several supplemental things I do to help clear my body, mind, and spirit when I'm not dancing. I'm a big believer in personal growth and continuous learning, so I read every day. I take courses, attend events geared toward self-actualization, and utilize the support of therapists, coaches, healers, and people who challenge my current line of thought. I approach healing with a knowing that I've employed ineffective coping mechanisms, I have a tendency toward co-dependency, and a pattern of controlling. For this reason, I find it particularly helpful to work with others who don't placate me but help me to see areas where I can improve. In other words, I appreciate people who recognize and call me on my bullshit. Any kind of growth I've experienced in my life has come from challenging my personal status quo. I recovered from depression because I questioned my repetitive negative thoughts and the doctors who told me I'd always suffer from depression and would require medication for the rest of my life. Jumping out of that paradigm and into a more healthful one didn't come naturally. It came from asking, *What if they're wrong? What if I have more power than I think? Where do I even begin? Who can help me in a more supportive, holistic way?*

Instead of anesthetizing distress with alcohol, drugs, food, sex, shopping, or other numbing agents, I'm learning to feel and dissolve discomfort. I've noticed that when I numb my pain instead of acknowledging and observing it, I give that pain new life. As a result, the pain will always resurface and often in more uncomfortable ways. I once was staying at an ex-beau's house and I proceeded to sleep-eat dog treats. Clearly something was wrong; I was masking pain and stuffing feelings on a whole other, unconscious level. It was a big wake-up call. It was time to get real and deal with the hurt instead of giving it new life. I allowed the truth I was stuffing to surface and I ended the unhappy twin trauma relationship.

In November of 2016, my Facebook friend, Sara Young offered free healing to anyone who needed energetic support. At the time, I was grieving the breakup. While I chose to end the relationship so I could pursue my dreams, I was missing the continuity of having a relationship, good sex, and a regular dance date in my life. I was also preparing for my biggest life change to date: selling my home and moving across the US. From our first call, it was obvious to Sara and me that I had an untapped power source I hadn't accessed. We've been working together consistently since that time, upping my ad hoc treatments to a weekly regimen for the last two years. Sara performs BodyTalk techniques to determine where my body needs attention. The energetic changes from BodyTalk are meant to restore communication within the body and jumpstart the its natural healing response. All of the work is done remotely while I sleep. The next morning, she sends an email confirming the state of my body when she checked in, the processes my body asked for, limiting beliefs that are hindering healing, and any intuitive hits she gets. As odd as all that all sounds, I've been in awe of the things she picked up, from anticipation in my system after an exciting first date, to trepidation about a work project, and even acknowledging I was drinking water with a rose quartz crystal in my water bottle. While I've tapped into my intuition greatly and go to great lengths to follow it, one of the major disconnects that interrupts this flow is an inability to stay grounded and in my body. This is something I'm specifically working on through BodyTalk. I appreciate Sara's work and the process that helps me recognize and heed subtle signals.

In 2017, Sara introduced me to breathwork as an integral part of our practice. I was 47-years-old before I understood the importance of proper breathing techniques. I was instructed to inhale through my nose to the count of five, and exhale through my mouth to a count of 10 or more. These deep breaths assist in resetting my nervous system to get me out of the near constant state of fight-or-flight I experience. The long exhale was really hard for me to do at first. When I think about it, it's not surprising to me. Most of my life, I "collected" experiences and emotions and rarely expressed them. An exhale is an expression, a release, which is the opposite of collecting. Releases are even more fun and powerful if you add sound to it. It's also a really effective way to release toxins from the body. It's a more subtle way to "flap your wings." Ilchi Lee, the man who founded Brain Education refers to breath work as, "a mind-body training method that helps each person create their own health, happiness, and peace." And he confirmed the significance of release in his book, *Connect*. Lee asserts that an exhale discharged through the mouth expels negative energy from thoughts and emotions to prepare you to experience your mind in your body, which is the first step in meditation.

It took me a long time to meditate because I was scared of it. I couldn't imagine having a clear mind, so I avoided meditation. Then, I worked with an extremely compassionate meditation teacher. He taught me that the practice was really about breath and presence. I learned, then, why the process was so hard for me. I have to be present and in my body to breathe properly. Also, when I breathe, I feel. Feeling my feelings scared me because I was used to repressing them. However, through meditation and breathwork, I learned I can effectively **release** painful feelings and even physical pain. I've even used breathwork to restore dangerously high blood pressure levels to normal.

More "standard" forms of support include massage, chiropractic care, and acupuncture. I've been working closely with massage therapists and chiropractors for decades. Acupuncture is new for me, but I enjoy it. Free Spin: insurance plans in California cover acupuncture and not chiropractic care—which is the opposite of Iowa plans.

Of course, some of my favorite ways to move energy include the use of crystals, lighting candles, burning incense, and smudging with sage or Palo Santo. I have an altar in my home where I display my treasures that help me focus and meditate. According to the website *Spirit Nest*, "Altars act as liminal space where the physical breaches the spiritual; where we can readily meet with Source Energy, the gods, our higher selves, angels, guides, and ancestors."

A creative and fun way to change energy is to use crystal yoni eggs. This is an egg-shaped crystal that's inserted vaginally. They help improve vaginal tone, which improves orgasmic response. In addition, different crystals provide different assistance. For example, I've cleared a migraine headache with a black obsidian yoni egg. When I first started using yoni eggs after my hysterectomy, they helped immensely in decreasing frequency to urinate and the awkward mishaps that sometimes happen with sneezes and ferocious laughter. Aside from the physical supports, yoni eggs provide energetic leverage as well. Once, I was dancing with a friend who looked at me and said, "Damn, you weren't fucking around getting ready tonight. You've got four auras going on!" In that moment, I realized I forgot to take my adventurine yoni egg out. After that experience, it's rare for me to dance without a yoni egg. (A large Adventurine yoni egg is pictured below. See the resource page at the end of this book for more details.)

Now that I'm remaining present on the dance floor, I no longer get hangovers. However, after a night of dancing, I often experience pain from hours of shaking my booty in high heels. In my "older" crowd at the club, many complain of knee and joint pain, too. I've found the best pain cream and CBD products designed to decrease inflammation and pain so I can dance more freely. (You can see the resource page for details on those, too).

As we talked about in chapter 19, the more connection points you have with a partner, the easier it is for the leader to lead and the follower to follow. The same is true with our bodies. Dance is one of the best ways to connect our body, brain, heart, and purpose. Even for me, that connection felt unnatural at first—especially after a lifetime of disconnection. Exploring additional points of self-connection whether that be through meditation, breathwork, yoga, crystal yoni eggs, sacred sexuality, or plant medicine, enhances our ability to navigate the dance floor and thus, the Dance of Life. Learning new skills, constantly expanding our repertoire, and remaining open to new opportunities makes dancing that much more fun.

[1] https://www.bodytalksystem.com/learn/bodytalk/

TranscenDANCE	
Dance through heartbreak and call in the supports you need for better health.	
TranscenDANCE statement:	There are many methods of connecting the body and mind, releasing emotions and optimizing health. Energy work, breathwork, and meditation are powerful tools for that.
TranscenDANCE prompt:	Breathe life into your Dance. Watch and follow this Body & Brain video on breathwork meditation: bit.ly/BodyBrainMeditation
TranscenDANCE Spotify playlist:	**Meditation** bit.ly/MeditationsPlaylist A fun mix of chill and energetic tunes for meditation.

We dance to seduce ourselves.
To fall in love with ourselves.
When we dance with another,
we manifest the very thing we
love about ourselves so that
they may see it and love us too.
—Kamand Kojouri

TranscenDANCE

Chapter 21

Dance Parties and Clubs

There's so much seduction, creativity, and playfulness on the dance floor. That's one of the reasons I love it—the energy is electric. I've always said dance floor energy is the best energy there is. I mean, you can't go wrong being in the presence of a disco ball, strobe lights, fake fog, and sweaty people expressing joy through body movement.

Since moving from Des Moines to the Los Angeles area, my options for dancing have expanded greatly. In Des Moines, most clubs were only open for dancing on the weekends. We were grateful to Mickey's and their midweek dancing on "college night." Our group of middle-aged moms had a great time starting, and often finishing, the dance festivities with patrons the same age as our kids. On a few occasions, my son and his buddies joined, and that was a blast. Most times though, we danced at Denny Arthur's feeling smug among an older crowd.

In California, I've come to appreciate ecstatic dance. It's free dance and movement with a DJ building up the energy and sometimes additional performers joining in. Ecstatic dance events are substance-free with a code of conduct that specifies no talking on the dance floor. There's a bit of seduction there, but the whole premise of ecstatic dance is that it's individual. It's meant to lead solo dancers back to their own seductive expression. There are no creepers and it's definitely not a place to pick someone up. Make friends? Sure.

There are many variations of dance communities in California, each with their own spin. There are even some that include plant medicine for the dance journey, which is a completely fun experience. Free Spin: There's legislation in California that allows organizations to register as a church in order to offer medicinal "sacraments" as part of their services. When I told my son about this, his reply was hilarious. He said, "I just found a new religion."

My first "club" experience in California was visiting the gay clubs in West Hollywood during my road trip. I literally couldn't get over all the sights. There were strippers everywhere! One thing I noticed last summer at the same clubs is the legality of marijuana and the ability to smoke on the patio. Back in the day, patrons used to be able to smoke cigarettes in the Iowa bars. I always showered before I got in bed because I couldn't stand the smell—especially in my bed. Oddly, the smell of pot is something I don't mind.

On the same road trip, I went to Parq in the Gaslamp District of San Diego. I was astounded by the sensory experiences of the club. The music was accompanied by a light show and Cirque-like performers scantily dressed doing acrobatic moves from rings that hung from the ceiling while confetti poured from above. Just when we were so hot we couldn't stand it, mist machines extinguished and refreshed us. The club includes a full-service **bar** in the women's restroom. As if women in the restroom aren't nice enough, add quick access to drinks with no line and no creepers, well, the conversations flowed readily, as you can imagine.

Another awesome experience I've done a few times with Xanadu Events, Co. is silent disco. Everyone wears a headset with three different channels. Three DJs spin different tracks on their respective channel and everyone dances to their own beat. It's like being in your own little world while also being in the energy of others. Like ecstatic dance, it's a substance-free zone and a more individualized experience. We had a silent disco party on the pier of Catalina Island at summer camp, which will go down as one of my favorite dance experiences ever. Free Spin: I also inadvertently found we can create our own, private silent disco experience. When I shared a house with other adults, I was wearing air pods dancing across the kitchen while my roommates watched and wondered what I was listening to.

In addition to the benefits of dance, non-club events like dance and movement classes cultivate friendships and grow tribes. I had a friend join me at Camp Xanadu. She asked me if I knew anyone else going to camp. I did not. However, I know what the organization stands for and the people attracted to those beliefs. I also had no question that I wanted more of those kinds of people in my life. Even going alone was a no-brainer for me. Also, these events are centered on personal reflection, individual integration, and collaboration. There's no posturing, pick-ups, or jealousy. Everyone is focused on their own journey, and that's a beautiful thing.

"This is a healing, it's not a competition."

Jeff, the instructor at movement class said the above as I was attempting, and failing, at putting my chin on my knee and completing other strange body configurations. During movement classes, the instructors often remind us to "respect body conditions" and modify the exercises to fit our needs. Because my body is wildly inflexible and oversized, that means I frequently do things differently than others—whether that's in yoga class or on the dance floor.

Moving differently than everyone else can be uncomfortable—when I'm comparing myself to others. On the other hand, when I think about how far I've come and focusing only on my personal healing, there's no discomfort—only pride.

I wondered what it would feel like if I approached life and dancing as a healing endeavor with focus only on my personal healing. I strongly believe we are here to heal ourselves and help others along the way. I need not worry about being ahead, falling behind, or getting down in a different position than others do. I can experience so much more self-compassion and motivation by focusing on my personal healing journey and how far I've come. I am my only competition.

<table>
<tr><td colspan="2">TranscenDANCE</td></tr>
<tr><td colspan="2">Go solo on new adventures and to new dance parties to connect with a like-minded tribe.</td></tr>
<tr><td>TranscenDANCE statement:</td><td>One path to creating TranscenDANCE is having an adventurous spirit and doing the unexpected!</td></tr>
<tr><td>TranscenDANCE prompt:</td><td>Solo Silent Disco: put on headphones and dance to your own party! (*Disco ball is optional.)</td></tr>
<tr><td>TranscenDANCE Spotify playlist:</td><td>On the Floor
bit.ly/OnFloorPlaylist

This is one of my favorite playlists ever. It’s full of dance tunes across all generations. If Denny Arthur’s had a soundtrack, this would be it!</td></tr>
</table>

To be creative means
to be in love with life.
You can be creative only if you
love life enough that you want to
enhance its beauty, you want to
bring a little more music to it,
a little more poetry to it,
a little more dance to it.
—Osho

TranscenDANCE

Chapter 22

Taking the Stage

Sometimes you have to clear the stage before you can take it.

The summer after delivering my TEDx Talk, I was in a deep depression. I had this expectation that after I delivered the talk, life would change in a big way. I planned to be traveling, speaking, and sharing "The Dance of Collaboration" with audiences all over the world. Except, nothing changed after the talk. Life wasn't moving forward at all. I reached out to so many therapists, coaches, readers, and healers in an attempt to discern and fix whatever my "problem" was. One person I connected with was an intuitive named Dana Machacek. She did a sacral chakra reading for me. According to MindValley, the "sacral chakra represents the very center of 'You.' The chakra originates from the Sanskrit word 'Svadhishthana,' which translates as 'one's own place' and refers to the true and untarnished aspects of the real you."[1] Orange is the color of the sacral chakra and it symbolizes pleasure, creativity, and enjoyment. I knew from previous experience that connecting to my own pleasure unlocked boundless creativity for me. At the time of the reading, though, I was very disconnected from pleasure and my center.

My disconnection was evident and clear. When Dana started reading my sacral chakra, she was overcome with emotion and immediately started crying. She described the images in her mind as a gaggle of giddy girls backstage. As the girls waited for their turn to take the stage, a tragedy unfolded before them. The star of the show was an elderly woman representing suffering, toiling, martyrdom, penance, purgatory, and anguish. Looking like the witch in *Snow White*, the decrepit actor onstage was holding all the power. Meanwhile, the young girls backstage waited in the wings for act two. Dana described the girls as gifts and aspects of me. She described them as joy, playfulness, creativity, juiciness, liveliness, vitality, sensuality, and connection. She noted the girls were made-up and decked out in ballet outfits. Except, they were put to the side while the onstage tragedy occurred.

Dana asserted that the girls' inability to take the stage was happening because my life was misaligned. She was not wrong. My life was incredibly out of balance and far from being aligned at this point. Even though my new life in California was completely unrecognizable from my depressive days in Des Moines, the anxiety of new experiences, feeling alone, and disappointment from my TEDx caused me to fall into some of my old, depressive patterns. I was doing the minimum to get by, emotionally eating, spinning my wheels during the day, and staying awake at night. In many ways, it was like the days gone by where I chased woke and begged sleep, only I didn't have the "luxury" of medication to assist and see me through.

I recognized the woman onstage as my mother. Honestly, I'm not sure if it really was my mother Dana saw. More likely, the idea of a decrepit, old witch onstage is more representative of the person I'd become if I didn't get my life in alignment, and fast. Dana further described the process of alignment as one that comes naturally when I am catapulted into joy, experience elation, and express profound gratitude. Joy, elation, and gratitude were severely lacking at that time. For nearly a year, I had been going through the motions of life, not getting much traction, and ignoring my joy. In other words, I was not aligned. Abraham Hicks often talks about alignment in the same way, describing the process of misalignment as vacuuming the carpet without plugging in the vacuum. That's kind of what my life felt like—looking good with clean carpet lines, but dingy and dirty under the surface.

Like the quiet mind that exists underneath the noise, those beautiful, little dancing girls were part of me. They'd just been waiting for the stage to clear as their cue to come and do their dance. The young ballerinas in the wings were ready. They giddily peeked out onstage. Dana described them further as cherubs who didn't feel fully allowed to take their space on the stage. She described the suffering, old woman as holding all the theatrical power and the girls—who represent creativity, gifts, hopes, dreams, and laughter—as not having any power. Or, more specifically, as not feeling they had any power. I myself felt this deeply as a child and even as an adult who was frequently out of place expressing such creativity, ingenuity, and intuitive abilities in a home or office environment where it wasn't safe to do so.

Dana began laughing wholeheartedly as she stayed tapped into the scene onstage, describing one of my spirit guides taking matters into her own hands: the old woman was quickly whisked off-stage with a Looney Tunes-style, oversized hook. The set was changed, props were placed, and the mood of the backdrop altered for the next act and a new beginning.

It was now time to make room onstage so the neglected and repressed aspects of me—the giddy ballerinas—could perform their dance. Even as Dana provided more details of these very personal aspects of me, my perfectionism began to rear its head, in real-time, as she was sharing with me. My ego began shunning the little girls for their emotion, their dramatics, their imperfections, and the way they enjoyed pleasure. She referred to the giddy girls as the innocent and untainted parts of me. These are the parts of me who access joy and alignment through laughter, play, skipping, jumping, and dance. These are the parts of me who trust without judgment, lack suspicion, have never been taken advantage of, been betrayed, or violated. The girls with their tutus and buns ready to take the stage are the way I played, laughed, and danced as a kid. Bigger than that, they represent the way I love. They're innocent. They're expressive. They're dramatic. They're unconcerned about what other people think. They're intuitive. In Abraham Hicks-speak, they are "tuned in, tapped in, and turned on." They just want to dance!

Here's why I shunned them: drama, expression, feeling, and intuition were unwelcome in my home. I was a "good girl" who was validated through perfectionism. These innocent girls didn't fit in the perfect world my ego repeatedly attempted to curate. Dana concluded her reading with some revelations for me. She said that, even in the midst of my brilliant transformation, I still wield a ball and chain; preventing change, preventing dancing. She said I had obviously grown, had spiritually expanded, and had been committed to my development. But like the old, bitter actress upstaging the ballerinas, my expectations kept me in purgatory, paying a penance, believing I'm not allowed to thrive. She remarked that I was fixated on a belief that I'm not allowed to thrive, and a fear that I'd be judged by others if I really soared like I intend to do; if I really took the stage like the giddy girls. Dana confirmed my suspicion that I was on the brink of massive change by noting I was on the precipice. The next part is where it gets interesting. She noted:

> What paves the way for your rise and for your launch and for your thriving is remembering and deciding that it's okay to be okay; that you can pledge allegiance to the highest and most fully expressed aspect of yourself rather than to the people or the crowds that you're trying to please and appease. Do right by her. And by her, I mean you. Honor her. Pledge allegiance to her, not to your past, not to perceived sins or flaws or fuck-ups, not to mistakes you made, not to people who might get upset or whose feathers will be ruffled if you stepped in. If you step into all of yourself, if you embody and express all of yourself, pledge allegiance to yourself, do right by you.

Dana remarked on the fierce energy of my spirit. She noted it's ferocious, empowered, and very aligned with no excuses, bullshit, apologies, or backing down. She finished with an invitation for me to do right by that spirit and help her to rise. Dana's message resonated strongly with me. Especially, "It's okay to be okay." So much of my anxiety is my own manufacturing. On some, deep-seated, egoic level, I'm more comfortable being uncomfortable. Discomfort is natural for me and I've spent a lot of my life in it. Joy is not as natural for me. I also have a hard time keeping a joyful perspective when others are struggling. I feel guilty for having a good life and rarely give myself proper credit for the sheer amount of work I've done to dig myself out of such a dark place, time and time again.

There's some beauty in the struggle. It's relatable. Who among us has not struggled in one way or another? Knowing someone else has overcome their life's obstacles is empowering. What I learned in a very deep way about struggle is the large amount of grief that's contained in letting go of it. For many, so much of our lives have been entrenched in one struggle or another. Our very identity is often tied up in our trauma. Letting go of the resistance, fighting ourselves, and stepping into our Divine worthiness and purpose also means releasing our own history. Including releasing many aspects, facets, and players associated with that history, like family members, friends, lovers, careers, possessions, and future aspirations. The grief can be so overwhelming, it keeps me stuck.

I'm finding that releasing the pain of my struggle and taking the stage in life is easier when I own my Divine worthiness. Every single person is born worthy. Yet, just like the giddy girls afraid to take the stage, I often have a hard time accepting and owning my worth. This one thing impacts everything from how I look, to what I do, to the people I relate with, to the things I attract, and the money I earn. Changing any of those things is predicated on alignment.

Growing up, I surmised that worthiness was earned by caring for others and putting them first. While suppressing and repressing my own needs, I went to great lengths to care for other people in an attempt to earn their love. This played out in a big way when my parents were dying and I cared for their nearly every need. I also "earned" worthiness through my career. At the same time, I was taught to downplay my success and hide my genius so others don't feel "less than," and not to be seen as a "bitch" or "know it all" by speaking up and expressing my ideas and needs.

Here's the thing about worthiness and unconditional love: it's inherent. I can honestly say I did not understand this until I was probably 35-years-old. I learned about unconditional love in a church service for young adults at Lutheran Church of Hope, a church I started attending when I was 26. When explaining God's love for us, Pastor Richard said, "There's nothing you can do to make me love you more, and there's nothing you can do to make me love you less." When you grow up trying to earn love and feeling like nothing you do will ever be enough, those words provided the biggest relief to me.

The thing is, giddy ballerinas don't question their worthiness. They're simply ready to share love onstage. They're focused on possibility, hope, and limitless potential. Without question, children own the worthiness that is inherently theirs. TranscenDANCE is a return to this state of *knowing*. It's knowing your worth, following the lead of the spirit guides who prepared the stage, daring to take the stage; all the while showcasing and entertaining as many other people as you can. I don't mean entertaining here as in "putting on a show," and people-pleasing your way to the stage. I mean vulnerably expressing yourself while engaging with others and helping them to see the light that exists within. Stepping onto the stage—the dance floor—of your life will bring light, energy, and arousal—which is what the sacral chakra is all about! Who doesn't love that?

Life's next act begins with one step. Having a grand life requires one to show up, step onto life's dance floor, and allow the Universe to take the lead. There's no need to perfect your form or choreograph every step along the way. Just take the floor. Life wants to dance with you. Close your eyes if you must, but please dance. When you're willing to own and express all that you are, the Universe will take you places you never imagined.

[1] https://blog.mindvalley.com/sacral-chakra/

TranscenDANCE

Take the stage and dance the expression of your own life.	
TranscenDANCE statement:	Clear the stage for your new alignment, freedom, creativity, and language of TranscenDANCE.
TranscenDANCE prompt:	Take your time getting ready to go out for a night on the town. Wear your best clothes, fix your hair and your face. Do everything that makes you feel good like you would when getting ready for a date. That can include a fresh shave, manscaping, or a saucy mani/pedi. When you're ready to take the stage, strut down your own catwalk. Better yet, make the next entrance to a public place your catwalk and STRUT!
TranscenDANCE Spotify playlist:	**Catwalk** bit.ly/CatwalkPlaylist This playlist is all about strutting your stuff and walking into places like you own them!

Those who were seen
dancing were thought to
be insane by those who could
not hear the music.
—Friedrich Nietzsche

TranscenDANCE

Chapter 23

The "Crazy" Rhythm of Life's Dance

As an aware and awake person who was previously unconscious, I hear music and frequencies other people tune out or don't hear. After awakening to several blaring pitches from the Universe, I'm now attentive to, trusting, and following the quiet tones. When I respond to these leads from the Universe, I do "crazy" things like buy a home as a single mother, abandon a successful, 25-year career, sell my home, and move across the country. I heed the Dance and take care of myself before other people. To be frank, me following the lead of the Universe hasn't always been met with support. In fact, more often than not, I'm met by people who can't hear the music telling me how crazy I am when I dance to the beat of my own drum.

"Crazy" is a word I used to own—quite affectionately, I might add. I made a home for the depressive disorders that shaped me and made me "crazy." I fought against the stigma of them, and I tried to keep them at bay with a cocktail of meds. The more I fought for these disorders, and against their stigma, the more I experienced them in greater degrees. In other words, I was attempting to make shit happen, by banishing the disorders from my experience, rather than accepting and *allowing* for greater health to ensue. I'm not sure how or why, but in late 2013, I decided to try something different. Instead of fighting for "crazy," I chose to fight for me. I banished the word "crazy" from my vocabulary and I fought for who I was as a person, thoughts and experiences that made me feel good instead of bad, and most importantly, I chose to fight for my joy. Joy is my birthright, after all.

And just like my mantra of "making shit happen," I realized that fighting for joy is the opposite of allowing it. When I fight for, and especially against something, I am controlling and can't be led. Imagine fighting for a dance! That's ri-damn-diculous. The Universe is always present, always available, and always down to boogie. I simply need to show up, be present and poised to respond to its lead, no fighting necessary.

Last summer, I spent an inordinate amount of time and money fighting for healing. I sought to banish my trauma—the crazy that resurfaced—and get my life on track. But doing this brought me to a new and different place regarding my crazy. Now, when I do things that feel crazy, I understand it as doing something that's different from what others anticipate, something that veers away from societal expectations, and something which is often incredibly creative. In other words, crazy is who I'm meant to be. Crazy is my zone of genius. Crazy is what makes me different from the sheep who follow the flock. Crazy is what makes the Dance in me come alive.

When I step out—especially when I step out boldly—others are often quick to judge. Here's what I know today: I'm not broken. I'm not "normal" either, but that doesn't mean normal is where it's at. Normal to me is just a setting on the dryer and nothing to aspire to. I was missing pieces of myself. I'm not missing these pieces because I am incomplete, but because I gave them away to others instead of keeping them for myself.

I lost a piece of myself every single time I swallowed my truth and subjugated my needs for the needs of others. I lost a piece of myself every time I didn't speak up and speak out. I lost a piece of myself every time I chose work over self-care. I lost a piece of myself every time my insecurity said "yes" when my body said "no." I lost a piece of myself every time I ignored my intuition. I lost a piece of myself every time I chose not to dance and live life. In order to feel and follow the lead of the Universe, I need to recognize, own, claim, and express my inherent power within. There's not a single thing wrong with me. Here's what's cooler: **what's true for me is also true for everyone**.

Like the greatest dance partners, the Universe helps you become more of yourself while also putting you in a position to showcase your skills. I absolutely love it when I'm dancing with Stephen and he opens a space for me to do a fancy turn. Sometimes he even remains still so the spotlight is totally on me as I dance. Even as I write this, "Never Gonna Let You Down" by Colbie Caillat is playing. The lyrics are a beautiful reminder of the way we are supported through this dance of life:

I'm always gonna build you up/And when you're feeling lost/I will always find you love/I'm never gonna walk away/I'm always gonna have your back/And if nothing else you can always count on that

I appreciate you reading this story of mine. I hope it helps begin a conversation on mental health and recovery through movement for you and yours. If you're struggling in the ways I did, please know that you're not alone and there's a way out that's as close as the dance floor. If you're not sure where to start, here are my top 10 tips:

1. **Remember who you are.** Know you are a child of God, no better and no worse than any other human on this planet. There's not a single thing wrong with you and you are no less deserving than any other human. The Universe is not discriminate when it comes to leading. Every single person is deserving of the Dance.

2. **Take care of yourself**. Be selfish. Carve out time for you and make it non-negotiable. Say "no" to things that cause you to compromise who you are. Say "yes" to things like dance that make you come alive.

3. **Feel your feelings and express them.** One of the greatest advantages of recovery is the ability to feel the highs and the lows of life, rather than the monotony of numbness. Dance and verbal expression are great ways to move emotion through your body.

4. **Get the support you need—whatever that looks like**. Also, understand that support looks different for every person. While I don't use meds now, they are an important part of my story and were required for many years. There's no shame or guilt in anything you need to get well. During the 20 years I was medicated, I spent a full seven years in bed. I was once asked why I took the meds, because they obviously didn't work. My reply was, "Yes, they did work. I'm alive." The world needs you and your unique, expressive dance. Bring your gifts to the dance floor and showcase them!

5. **Please understand that every experience—no matter how traumatic—is a gift**. It's possible to look at our experiences for the blessings they bestow. When we learn to express gratitude and appreciation for life's highs **and** lows, the Universe reveals lessons—like dance lessons—which unveil even more gifts. For example, as painful as my critical illnesses were to experience, they led me to dance and dancing is one of the greatest gifts I've ever, ever known.

6. **Act on the inspiration you receive—no matter how crazy it feels or how crazy it appears to others**. This is your intuition talking and it's never wrong. It's a lead from the Universe and you don't want to miss any dances.

7. **Know that everything is a process.** As I shared before from Abraham Hicks, "You can't get it wrong and you

never get it done." Sometimes we take detours—like spending seven years in bed—but your destiny is alive and will bloom in perfect timing. While we're here, we should dance.

8. **Get a therapist, coach, mentor, or friend to help you stay accountable**. While there's value in spending time alone to ensure you're resonating with your own intentions and not the prescriptions of others, we get well in community and with the support that helps us stay on track. A supportive, inclusive dance community with regularly scheduled events is a great way to be accountable.

9. **Fuck what they think**. Wayne Dyer had it right when he said, "What other people think of you is none of your business." No one has the same heart or the same inspiration as you. No one else can express your dance in the same way you can. If people judge or shame your actions, remember that being on the dance floor is the equivalent of being in the arena of life. Feedback from critics—especially critics who are not in the arena—doesn't count.

10. **Never stop dancing.** Dance through the heartbreak and dance to bring joy. Dance with different partners, and dance alone. Dance through life and stay loyal to the Universe as the greatest dance partner there is.

Keep in mind that "wellness" and "what works" don't look the same to everyone. Neither does "crazy." I believe crazy is who we are trying to be birthed. Crazy is the dance within. Bringing that dance to life in the following ways may be negatively interpreted by bystanders who can't hear the music. That's okay; do them anyway:

- Take the stage and dance the expression of your own life.
- Go solo on new adventures and to new dance parties to connect with a like-minded tribe.
- Dance through heartbreak and call in the supports you need for better health.
- Refuse to settle for dance partners and life partners who don't have all the connection points you need.
- Remember to recognize the progress and subtle turns that aren't wildly obvious.
- Live your truth and let intuition lead; allow shit to unfold.
- Open yourself up to new tunes and genres of music as you evolve.
- Take new dance classes, feel foolish when you're challenged by the choreography, and refuse to quit.
- Follow your joy to a state of flow.
- Do the work to meet your partner in the middle while your partner does the same.
- Stay rooted in your truth; but be uninhibited and accept directional nudges as they arrive.
- Place yourself in a target-rich environment for your future self—even if that means moving across the country.
- Support others to be their best selves.

- Jump into the middle of someone else's dance circle and get down.
- Surrender control and let someone else lead.
- Accept dances, friendships, and lovers without leaping immediately to attach to them.
- Tune into and respect your body's "Yes."
- Pause to take a breath.
- Pivot so you can travel in new directions.
- Accept sensitivity as the gift that it is.
- Be and express your whole self; and accept every part of your story—especially the chapters you wish you could hide.
- Be present and available for the inevitable lead of the Universe.

Every week, when I go to dance lessons, Stephen takes my hand and we walk in-step to the dance floor. I have no idea what's coming, but I trust I will have fun, I will learn new things, and I'll get to practice things I've learned before. I'm certain I'll screw up, we'll laugh, and we'll keep dancing. I follow his lead without question because I know that even if the worst thing happens—I step on his toes, I fall down, I can't keep up—I know I'm not alone. I know Stephen will help me, and he'll do everything in his power to help our movements evolve as beautifully and naturally as possible, while presenting me in the best possible light.

It's exactly the same way with the Universe. The Universe wants to see us shine. The moon is a great disco ball in the sky and the Universe has an outstretched hand ready to lead you on the dance floor of life. Keep your eyes on the vision among the stars you've already prepared, knowing not everyone has the same view as you, nor can they hear the same music. That's totally okay. You see, lastly, crazy is accepting the lead from the Universe when it offers you a hand in the dance of life and asks you to step into the unknown with the greatest faith you've ever known.

Promise me you'll give faith
a fighting chance;
And when you get the choice
to sit it out or dance—
I hope you dance.
—Lee Ann Womack

TranscenDANCE

TranscenDANCE Resources

TEDx:

The Dance of Collaboration (bit.ly/MDrakeTEDx)

Books:

Gabby Bernstein, *Super Attractor: Methods for Manifesting a Life Beyond Your Wildest Dreams*

Kyle Cease, *The Illusion of Money: Why Chasing Money is Stopping You from Receiving It*

Ilchi Lee, *Connect: How to Find Clarity and Expand Your Consciousness with Pineal Gland Meditation*

Dr. Bradley Nelson, *The Emotion Code: How to Release Your Trapped Emotions for Abundant Health, Love and Happiness*

Robert Scheinfeld, *Busting Loose from the Money Game: Mind-Blowing Strategies for Changing the Rules of a Game You Can't Win*

Regena Thomashauer, *Pussy, A Reclamation*

Coaches:

Dance Instructor, Stephen Thomas (www.stephenthomasdance.com)

BodyTalk Practitioner, Sara Young (www.spikeofalltrades.com)

Intuitive Counselor and BioMat distributor, Rita Henry (www.ritahenry.com)

Sacral Chakra Reading, Dana Machacek

Events:

Camp Xanadu (campxanadu.org)

Ecstatic Dance Los Angeles (ecstaticdancela.com)

Retail Products:

Gemstone Crystal Yoni Eggs, Gemstone Yoni (bit.ly/BrilliantYoniEggs)

CBD Oil Formulated for Pain and Inflammation, CTFO (bit.ly/MD10xGold)

Deep CBD Healing Pain Cream, CTFO *(bit.ly/MDPain)*

Visit uncorpedinfluence.com for downloadable dance memes, Spotify playlists, and related published articles.

You dance love, and
you dance joy, and
you dance dreams.
—Gene Kelly
TranscenDANCE

CPSIA information can be obtained
at www.ICGtesting.com
Printed in the USA
BVHW041925030420
576812BV00008B/326

9 781734 654318